ELDORADO

ELDORADO

My Childhood During the Great Depression

MARGARET WENTZEL LIPTHAY

authorHOUSE®

AuthorHouse™
1663 Liberty Drive
Bloomington, IN 47403
www.authorhouse.com
Phone: 1-800-839-8640

Published by AuthorHouse   05/21/2012

ISBN: 978-1-4685-7309-1 (sc)
ISBN: 978-1-4685-7308-4 (e)

Library of Congress Control Number: 2012905471

Any people depicted in stock imagery provided by Thinkstock are models, and such images are being used for illustrative purposes only.
Certain stock imagery © Thinkstock.

This book is printed on acid-free paper.

DEDICATION

In memory of my beloved parents

Grete and Ernst Wentzel, who gave me a wonderful childhood.

Thanks also to my many friends and family members who have helped me with this book, mostly computer help, as I am totally computer illiterate;

Dotty Dine, Michele Stromer, Kim Takvorian, Barbara & Gary Mc Cray, Mel Markward, the Computer Club of Century Village.

My thanks also to my Internet researchers, Barbara Mc Cray and Jane McAllister Yantis, (baby sister of George McAllister, who was a classmate in Eldorado.) Thanks also to my friends in George Bettinger's writing class for all their encouragement, and especially my friend, Carol Hinton, who insisted that I must write this book because she enjoyed my stories about the farm so much. I sincerely hope I have not omitted anyone.

2. Lori on handles of wheelbarrow, Margaret inside, City Island, 1928

13. Margaret Lipthay, 2012, working at cat shelter

3. In the canoe, Ernst Wentzel, Adolf Gaub, Greta Wentzel,
Lori Gaub, Margaret, unknown dog.
City Island, 1929

1. Greta Wentzel and her daughters, Margaret and Lori, Hamburg 1927

10. Recycled smokehouse, Adolf Gaub, Dina the dog, Margaret and Ernst Wentzel

11. Ellie Gaub, petting Dina, Margaret in back and Ernst Wentzel

12. Ellie, Annemarie & Rosemarie Gaub, 1942, Margaret Wentzel, Astoria, 1939

4. Lori and Elinore Gaub, City Island, 1932

5. Porch in Maryland, Aunt Grete and Margaret, 1932

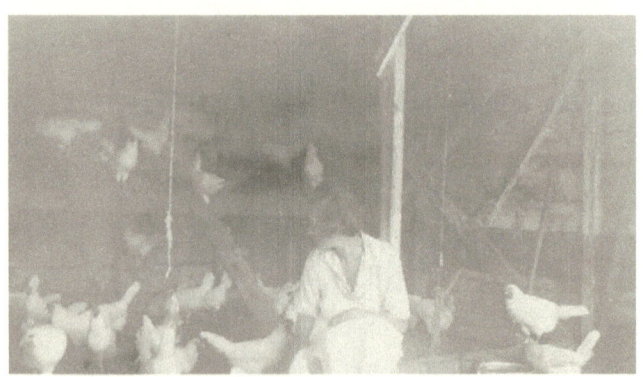

7. Greta and chickens 1932

6. Margaret and chickens, 1932

8. Oscar Beabout feeding calf and Margaret, 1933

9. Ernst Wentzel, Lori Gaub, Margaret Wentzel, Ellie and Adolf Gaub,
with his car, 1935

CHAPTER 1

THE FARM ON THE EASTERN SHORE

"Deti", my father said, "Don't play in the shade. It's much too cold. Stay in the sun, keep warm and don't catch another cold". I sighed. I knew that he was right, I was very prone to catching colds. Still, I didn't like the idea of playing in the sun. The whole point of the game was to slither around on the frozen puddles, which had of course melted in the sunny areas. I did what I was told, kept sighing and standing around in the sunshine, and looking unhappy. I was not so sure that I was going to like living in this new place at all.

Papa had been here for a month when Mama and I came down from New York to the Eastern Shore of Maryland. It was January, 1931, and my father had been very worried about the Depression and how long it was going to last. There was just no work available, not for anyone and certainly not for him. He had been making very upscale, expensive gold jewelry, and there was no longer demand for luxuries like that now. He had been out of work for over a year now and felt that he must do something soon to secure our future as best he could. He had taken the savings he had left, $1000, and set out to buy a farm, thinking that at least we could always have something to eat. It was a good thought, but the only experience he had with farming had been when he was five years old and his widowed father had sent him to spend his summers with his uncle, who, himself, was only a part-time farmer because he spent the winters teaching school! Not a whole lot of experience for Papa, but he was always optimistic. "How hard could it be?" He soon found out!

My parents had looked at a farm in upstate New York first. I remember sailing up the Hudson River on the Day Line with them to look at one such farm. About the farm itself, I remember nothing, but I'll never forget the house, especially the living room. I had never seen flypaper before and when I saw those long spirals of sticky yellow paper hanging from the ceiling, I was shocked, even at five years of age, because I didn't realize that their purpose was to catch flies and not to be some sort of decoration. Ugly! Anyway my parents didn't buy that farm, but probably not because of the flypaper.

Years later, on the farm, we had flypaper of our own, still unattractive to me, but apparently not to the flies, as there were plenty of them stuck to it. We had house guests once, who brought their cat "Flinty", named for the city of her birth, Flint, Michigan. She was a regal longhaired Persian who did not associate with our cats and stayed indoors. The flypaper caught her attention one day and she thought it might make an interesting plaything and jumped off the buffet to grab that intriguing spiral which was twisting over her head. Big mistake! Cat and flypaper became hopelessly entangled. It took four adults to separate the yowling and clawing cat from the flypaper.

But back to the farm, it consisted of 33 acres, most of it pine woodlands. It was located in Dorchester County on the banks of the Marshyhope Creek, which was not a creek. It was actually a tide water river, about 75 feet across, and deep enough for fairly large boats to navigate, although very few did. Before the repeal of Prohibition, bootleggers would bring their cargo up the river by boat at night, stop at our place and transfer it to waiting trucks. My father's role in this enterprise was to leave a lantern lit on the decrepit dock that remained at the edge of the river, left over from the busier days of the roaring twenties. The next morning a bottle of whiskey had mysteriously appeared on our front porch! Repeal killed this endeavor, even though Dorchester remained a "Dry" County. There just wasn't enough business left to continue.

CHAPTER 2

SCHOOL DAYS

Even though we moved to Maryland in January of 1931, and I was to start school in February in New York City, I didn't. I did not mind this one bit, I had more time to play. Classes in Maryland began in September and ran until June. There were no A and B sessions. In City Island, I was ready to be promoted out of Kindergarten in February and would have been enrolled in 1A at that time. I had already been introduced to the teacher, a Mrs. Byrd. To my great disappointment, no way did she look anything like a bird! My mother had received a postcard from the school when I was four, at that time too young for Kindergarten, to come and enroll me anyway, so that I could get a headstart on learning to speak English. My mother, my sister, Lori, who was nineteen at the time and I had emigrated from Hamburg, Germany in 1928 to join my father, who had arrived the year before. Economic conditions were in shambles in Germany at that time, and it was almost impossible for anyone to make a decent living. My father was still suffering from the two severe wounds he received during the first World War. In addition the political situation did not look good and did not seem to be getting better. His plan was, emigrate to America where everyone makes lots of money and then, if things looked better, both economically and politically, go back to Germany. Of course, this never happened for several reasons.

We arrived in New York on my third birthday. I remember it clearly. Papa met us at the dock in a taxi. It was raining and he had brought me a little red plaid umbrella. It's strange that I remember the cab ride to

3

City Island so well and recall nothing about the ship "New York" that we had just disembarked. In later years, my mother filled me in some of the details of our trip. Even though it had been a relatively calm crossing, my sister and mother had gotten very seasick, and had no interest in food and did not want eat breakfast and just wanted stay put in the cabin until they felt better. Not me, though! I had been befriended by a group of teenagers who thought I was cute. So at breakfast time, I insisted that I must go down to the dining hall, because my friends were expecting me! From then on, Mama would tell everyone, "My Deti never gets seasick!" It was tough sometimes to live up to that, but if your mother says you never get seasick, by golly, you never do get seasick! Years later when I was married, my husband said he was the envy of his friends. Their wives did get seasick and refused to accompany them on fishing trips.

Getting back to our arrival in New York, my father had rented an apartment for us on City Island, in the extreme far reaches of the Bronx, New York City. This was about as far away from Manhattan as you can get and still be within the confines of New York City. At the end of the IRT Pelham Bay Line there was a bus that crossed several bridges and wound up in City Island. At the far end of Ditmars Street was our apartment on the second floor, accessible only by an outside stairway which went up on one side and down on the other. This apartment had evidently been converted from an original one-family home, which now consisted of two apartments. There was no actual bathroom. A hall closet in the living room had a toilet, and another closet in the bedroom contained a shower. However, the apartment did have a very nice view. From the porch, which was neither enclosed or screened, Long Island Sound could be seen spread out and covered with countless boats, anchored or sailing all summer long.

When we arrived, my father had a red tricycle waiting for me for my third birthday. Super surprise, as I had not seen my father in over a year and did know what to expect. The very next day, Mama said to me, "You should take your tricycle downstairs and meet the children in the neighborhood" I did this, went downstairs with my new red tricycle, and returned shortly thereafter, laughing uproariously. Mama said, "Why did you come back so soon, and what could have been so terribly funny to make you laugh so much?" When I finally regained my composure, I said, "You would not believe how funny those kids are. I have never seen this,

I talk to them, and they seem to be answering, but I can't understand a word they are saying. They just go on and on, talking and talking and making no sense!" She started to laugh as well, "I guess I should have warned you that you might have trouble understanding them, I thought kids get along O.K. with just some kind of kid communication. They are speaking English, and you will too, very soon". This was a revelation to me. I had no idea that everyone did not speak German as we did. I was totally unaware that other languages existed, as I had never heard any before. My mother kept her promise. The very next day, she took me to the library to get books and began reading to me in English. This must have been kind of slow going at first because she herself was not that proficient in English. But she was a very determined lady and her daughters deserved the very best she could possibly give them.

I learned to communicate with the neighborhood kids pretty fast, so that by the time I was summoned to register for kindergarten, I was able to get along quite well, with only a few glitches. For example, for Thanksgiving, we were all supposed to color the paper turkey cutouts that were to be used to invite our parents to the holiday celebration at the school. I had no idea what a turkey was. Had never seen one, certainly never ate one, so I asked my teacher, Mrs. Dill, what color turkeys were. She said, without seeming to give it much thought, "All colors". I used every crayon in my box of crayons to color that turkey. I did not like that look at all. It just looked pretty much the way one would have expected, using that method, a mess! On another occasion, I fared much better. In class, for whatever reason, I don't remember, we drew little pictures in designated squares on a sheet of paper. I brought it home, and as it was a rainy afternoon and I was confined indoors, I cut apart the little squares and sewed them together to make a little book. It was this effort that so impressed Mrs. Dill that she took me and introduced me to the aforementioned Mrs. Byrd. (she of the unbirdlike characteristics] In all probably a lot of four and five year-olds do not hear or grasp the words of various songs and just sing along what they actually do hear, as they do not have very extensive vocabularies, either. I know I did. I sang about the the jingle bells on the one horse SOAP and sleigh. One of my favorites was "Three CHAIRS for the Red, White and Blue". I envisioned the three colored stripes, each sitting on it's own chair. It was a very nice picture and made as much sense to me as a lot of other words did.

I never played with the toys or books that belonged to the kindergarten. The toys were very, very worn and did not look clean to me. I very much preferred to play with my own. And, as for the books, they were all marked up and had been scrawled in. That was a definite no-no at our house! As I had been taught never, ever to write in, or mark up a book, I was careful not to even touch them, as I did not want to be found guilty by association. I was very cautious at a very early age!

September rolled around, inevitably. Time for me to start the first grade in Eldorado. School was nothing new to me. I had, of course, attended kindergarten in City Island and nursery school in Hamburg, Germany, when I must have been about two years old. I have no memory of that. My mother was busy selling off the remaining merchandise that my father had left when he went to America, and Mama felt that she would not be able to devote enough time to me and thought I would be happier with children my own age. I disagreed and would have enjoyed staying home. In fact, considering how much nursery school was costing her, she whole-heartedly agreed with me and took me out. The teacher there had given her some of the things I had supposedly crafted, but even Mama who thought her girls could do just about anything, was skeptical. "No two-year old ever wove a paper mat like that by herself", she said. But as it was kind of pretty, it was sent to New York as Papa's birthday gift from me.

In Maryland, I went to school in the nearest town, called Eldorado [one word, Delmarva pronunciation, not El Dorado, Spanish pronunciation]. The school consisted of four rooms, but only three were used as classrooms. The fourth had a sliding wall so that it could be converted into one large room by combining it with the adjacent room and thus become the auditorium. One room was a classroom for the first and second grades. Mrs. Rodgers taught them. My first year in each classroom was interesting. I would listen to the teacher work with my class, but when she went on to teach the other class, I, of course, kept right on listening, absorbing their lessons as well. This was fine except that I rarely completed the busy work that I was supposed to be doing on what I had just learned in the previous class. This consisted of just writing endless columns of numbers. My homework was also writing down these numbers. This was far from exciting. I had learned to count in kindergarten! The second year in any classroom was excruciating. I had learned every bit of that stuff the previous year and had absolutely no interest in hearing it all over again, despite the fact that it was what I was supposed to learn now! Regardless, I did well in school. My parents were very proud that I, as a foreigner, got the highest mark in English.

And so it went. The third grade was in another room, taught by a Miss Moore. The third grade was interesting. All new to me. When I entered the fourth grade and had to listen to all those facts again, boredom set in once more. After surviving the fourth grade, I once again entered a new room for the fifth grade. It was a nice challenge. But here there was a new twist. The fifth, sixth and seventh grades were all in this one room which was taught by Mrs. Taylor, who was also the principal of the school. I now had two classes to listen to while I was supposed to be doing my work. No chance that ever got finished!

There were some strange rules in this school. To this day I do not understand why, for instance, no one was permitted to wear a sweater in the classroom, no matter how cold it was. One of the boys tried to hide a sweater by wearing it under his shirt, got caught and was subsequently paddled. I really could not see how that was such an awful offense, other than that he knew it wasn't allowed. Corporal punishment was fairly routine there, for the boys anyway. I don't recall any girls getting paddled. They must have been better behaved or smart enough not to get caught.

There was a large wood-burning stove in each room which had a stamped tin mantle surrounding it, probably to keep young arms and legs from getting too badly burned upon contact. Desks near the stove were comfortable enough, but in cold weather, away from the stove and closer to the door, it could get bitterly cold. Mama got tired of my constant colds and tried to do something about it. She walked the whole distance to the school, about six or seven miles to complain. My teacher was sympathetic, but all she was able to do was change my desk to one nearer to the stove. Still no sweaters permitted! Another time my mother walked all the way to Eldorado to inquire why I had received a "D" in arithmetic, even though my father had just recently commented to her that he was pleased that I was doing so well. It turned out that I had missed too many tests because I was absent because I had a cold. Sometimes you just can't win!

CHAPTER 3

ELDORADO

Eldorado Grammar School was located in a square brick building which had been built some time in the late 1920s. It had white wooden columns out front and looked very nice and impressive. The original school building had burned down some time earlier, probably in the early 1920s. I never got the whole story. The older kids would sort of give out little bits of information, but I really don't know what actually happened, if any lives were lost or even the cause of the fire. There were rumors that mice had chewed on matches and ignited them. Again no conclusive information. There must have been a fire house somewhere in the area, although I don't know where. There had to be. Every summer a Firemen's Carnival was held in Sharptown, in the next county, Wicomico. This was a very big social event. Everybody came. There was a carousel, Ferris wheel and all sorts of games and contests designed to separate the patrons from their spare cash. You just had to be seen there! People dressed up for the occasion and wore their best Sunday clothes. My sister and her family had come down from New York once while this celebration was going on. Lori, my sister, had no idea what a big deal this was for the neighbors and thought it would be appropriate to wear slacks. Slacks were just coming into style at that time, perhaps 1934, and had never been seen on ladies in the neighborhood and folks were shocked! Women and girls might wear overalls if they were doing heavy farm work, but never, ever if they were going to any sort of affair. My sister, of course, knew nothing about this, coming from New York, and blithely wondered why people were staring at her. I knew, but was too embarrassed to tell her! Besides, she wouldn't have gone home to change anyway, especially in view of the fact that home was about ten miles away!

Eldorado School was modern enough to have electric lights, but no running water, and surely no telephone! Water was supplied by a hand pump which was situated in the tower, under the bell. We were encouraged to wash our hands and carefully dispose of the paper towels in the waste basket. This pump was also our source of drinking water. We were all supposed to bring in our own drinking cup and not borrow our friends'. As this cup was usually forgotten at home, it behooved us to quickly pump the water several times, quickly cup our hands under the spout and drink as fast as possible. Doing this two or three times usually satisfied our thirsts. On one occasion a telephone might have been nice to have. Two of the boys were horsing around and the bigger one picked up the smaller one. Unknown to anyone, the bigger boy was epileptic, had an episode at that exact moment, dropped the smaller one to the ground and broke his leg! It was up to the principal to take the injured boy to the doctor. She was gone all afternoon. We all survived including the boy with broken leg, who appeared in class a few days later, on crutches. These were greatly admired. Blood and bandages and any medical items are always interesting to children. I remember once I had helped my dad load sweet potatoes on to a horse drawn sled he had made. It got late and we had to come home in the dark. Therefore I attributed the stickiness of my hand to the juice of the sweet potatoes. Imagine my surprise and shock when I walked into the kitchen, and discovered that it was actually blood! I had been holding on to the single-tree, the gadget on the front of the sled through which the horse's lines lead to her bit, and somehow it had cut my hand rather deeply. Of course it wasn't a serious problem for Mama because she had been a nurse.

She bandaged it up expertly and everything was fine. However, at school the next day, just about all the kids wanted to see it. They wanted me to take off the bandage so that that they could get a better look at it, but I would not relent. My mother would have been furious!

The toilets were located at the ends of the shed where the teachers parked their cars, the girls' at one end and the boys' at the other. These were, of course just fancy outhouses, three seaters, also without running water. Emptying them daily was just one more of the janitor's jobs, as well as supplying wood for the stoves and keeping them ignited in cold weather, and keeping the school neat and clean. There was also a library, located in the room with the higher grades. Before I left Eldorado, I had just about read every book in it. That may sound impressive or boastful, but it is really neither. This library consisted of one bookcase, smaller than the one we had at home. My parents were constantly urging me to read their German books, but I always went for the English books first. I very much preferred them to the German books which were all very old and printed in old German script. It was like reading old English script, but much harder. As I had never read enough German to have word recognition skills, I was compelled to sound out almost every word. I had an awful lot of trouble distinguishing between different capital letters, A and U; B and V; C, E and G looked almost alike to me. I had to apply each capital to the front of the lower case letters, which I had no trouble with, to see if it made a word I recognized. As every noun is capitalized, it was extremely slow going. Is it any wonder that I much preferred reading English books!

It was necessary to acquire a considerable amount of manual dexterity in Eldorado School. A frequently used punishment was to be assigned to write out each corrected test answer one hundred times. This was obviously a drag, so the accepted, not by the teacher, naturally, method was to write with two or three pencils in one hand and not get caught. I was quite good at this and never got caught. Once, I was caught at another misdeed and had to sit in the corner. It turned out to be a fulfilling experience. My class was sitting around in a circle and reading aloud from one of our text books. As a good portion of the kids didn't read all that well, I was bored. I began to read quietly to myself, ahead of the rest of the class, when my teacher noticed me carefully turning the pages. She was greatly annoyed and made me sit in the corner, without my book, unfortunately. I was vindicated when she started asking questions about the material we had just read, and no one knew the answer except me. I felt very smug and gleeful.

Getting back to the water situation, a lady once came to our school who evidently was representing Lifebouy Soap, as she gave each of us a tiny bar of their soap, about the size of a hotel soap bar. I found them to be extremely cute, as I had never seen such tiny soaps. My mother made her own soap from spare grease and lye and did not cut them into such tiny pieces. They were beyond a doubt adult soap bars! Once she must have stirred the mixture a bit longer than usual and wound up with soap which floated, just like Ivory soap. The Lifebouy lady gave us a lecture on the use of soap. Always wash our hands before meals and after using the bathroom, and take at least one bath a week! With Lifebouy Soap, of course. It sounds hilarious today, but in those days it seemed perfectly acceptable and not funny and nobody laughed. There were some children who could have benefitted from this information, but I doubt if they did. There was a family of three girls and a boy in our school who had lost their mother and were being raised by their father who was doing a terrible job. What money he could scrape together, he promptly gave to his church and spent almost nothing on his kids and neglected them as well. I felt even then, as I do today, charity is fine, but should really begin at home. His kids went to school dressed in dirty, ragged clothes and smelled really bad. They were certainly not popular and had no friends. I felt very sorry for them, but did not know how to help. I suppose I could have shared my lunch with them, as they probably didn't get enough to eat either, but I didn't have enough for five. Besides, there were aggressive kids in the school who were already willing to con me out of my sandwich! Today it seems inconceivable that the authorities did not step in to help, but no one did. It is unlikely that the father would have accepted help of any sort. A lady in Sharpetown tried to adopt one of the younger girls, but the father would not hear of it. Those kids were total permanent outcasts. Even the teachers showed little compassion. The oldest girl was named Helen and one of the teachers renamed one of the book characters she was reading to us about, "Helen-Suck-Her-Thumb" instead of the original name of the thumb sucker. Perhaps she thought she was helping Helen, but it didn't work. Helen continued to suck her thumb. I would have too!

CHAPTER 4

THE FARMHOUSE

When my mother got her first look at the farmhouse, which was to be our new home in Maryland, she almost went into shock. She said to my father, "How could you have possibly picked out this place to be our new home? Every house that we both looked at was nicer than this place! I knew that it was a mistake to send you out by yourself to find us a place to live!" Even though she had not expected much in the way of amenities, knowing my father and his ideas, but this was unbelievable! There were holes in the walls, some of the windows were broken and none of them would stay open without being propped up with a stick. The sash cords were non-existent. The woodwork had undoubtedly never been painted since the house had been built, sometime in the 1890s. It seemed to have built in two sections. The West Wing, if I may use such a pretentious term, had probably been constructed first. It consisted of two fairly large rooms, one downstairs and one upstairs connected by a reasonably nice stairway. Later, an addition had been attached. It had two rooms downstairs, one of which was the kitchen, and two rooms upstairs with very low ceilings which were never used for anything besides storage, except once, when the hen house being used for baby chicks at the time, caught fire and started to smolder. The chicks were quickly gathered up, in pillowcases and aprons and whatever else could be found and quickly transferred to the empty upstairs bedroom. They were none the worse for their adventure! The two rooms downstairs were used as a dining room when we had company, and the kitchen. Of course, we had no electricity and never did get it, as it was much too expensive to have a line laid to our house, which was way back in the woods. Our water supply, for those days, was really quite up-to-date. The hand-operated pump was actually in the kitchen, not out in the yard where most folks had theirs. This really didn't impress my mother very much.

The rest of the plumbing consisted of an outhouse out back which was customary. Taking a bath was cumbersome. First the water had to be heated in a kettle on the wood-burning range, then poured into the laundry tub which was placed in the middle of the kitchen floor at bath time. Baths were carefully scheduled, no unnecessary ones were taken. To do the laundry, Mama put this same laundry tub on the stove and boiled the clothes for a while. If they needed more attention, which they usually did, she got out the washboard, applied her homemade soap, and started scrubbing! It was not an easy life for her. My father, however, thought it was a great piece of property, the best he had seen. It had such a wonderful view, right on the river, woods all around us, and so quiet, far away from the hustle and bustle of the city. If he noticed the house at all, it was just to verify that there was one. He thought it was so great. Mama, on the other hand, did not. She was a very meticulous housekeeper and this would be the ultimate challenge. Something she had never expected. She kept repeating, "Ernst, what have you gotten us into?"

The house and the tillable fields lay far back in the woods, accessible only by two dirt roads leading back from State Road #313. These roads were probably about one-half mile apart. The more commonly used one had an enormous puddle which never dried up. It had to be navigated by staying as far to the left as possible. If anyone ventured too far to the right with his vehicle, it was almost sure to get stuck in the mud. It was impossible to go around it, the trees grew right up to the road. It was kind of tricky. The lesser used road was very, very sandy, so driving on that was no picnic, either, but as we had no car, it wasn't important to us. The school bus came down on 313 and kids had to be by the highway to get picked up. It was about a mile and a half on either of these dirt roads to reach the highway from our house, but my parents would absolutely not hear of me walking it by myself. One of them, mostly my mother always accompanied me. Our mailbox was also at the pick-up spot. Our official address was Rhodesdale, Md., but we lived nowhere near Rhodesdale. That was where the nearest railway depot was. Letters and small packages were delivered by the mailman from his car. Any large shipments had to be picked up by the recipient at the depot.

Sometime during the thirties, my father came home very excited and said, "Greta, the mailman has a new car, and, would you believe, it does not have to be cranked by hand to start the engine! He just turns a key and the car starts, like magic". It was probably the first self-starting car in the neighborhood. Everyone else had old, old cars that required a lot of cranking to get started. Sometimes it worked, other times not. Sometimes, the crank reversed its self and flew backwards and broke the guy's arm. Even though gas was very cheap in those days, as my husband always told me, eight gallons for a dollar, it didn't mean that tanks were always kept filled. Even a dollar was sometimes very hard to come by during the Depression. One of my father's friends had a truck and he took the three of us for a ride. He had to cross a bridge to Vienna, across the Nanticoke River. There just wasn't enough gas in the tank to get across, as the uphill ride pushed it in the wrong direction. After several unsuccessful attempts, he hit upon the solution; cross the bridge in reverse! And so he did without further problems. Once the truck was over the hump, gravity would take it down the other side. This fellow, Alex worked for a restaurant whose owner was replacing his Victrola because it had a broken spring. I was to be the lucky recipient of this Victrola with the broken spring, which required almost constant winding to keep it going, as well as some records, 78s of course, the only kind available. Years later, back in New York, my girlfriends and I still danced to these records; Glenn Miller, Benny Goodman, and Tommy Dorsey, still taking turns winding the Victrola. On the farm it had been such a wonderful gift, I could listen to music anytime I liked! We lived so far back in the woods that I never could have friends over, and not having siblings near my own age at home, I was a very solitary child. It didn't bother me, I could always amuse myself, even before I had the Victrola, but my mother worried. Children should have playmates, not always be alone, reading or playing with the animals. Her point of view was quite understandable, as she was the youngest of thirteen children.

My father, the ultimate recycler, kept the old Victrola in our basement in New York long after we had an electric phonograph. He finally found the time to use the wood to make me a curio cabinet, which is still in my living room today.

CHAPTER 5

THE ANIMALS

Every Farm needs animals. They are part of the décor, in addition to being vital to self-sustainment. About the first to arrive at our farm were the chickens. Unbelievably enough, the baby chicks were ordered by mail from Sears Roebuck. They were one day-old chicks and came in perforated corrugated boxes of 100. These boxes were about three or four inches high and probably about two feet square. My father had ordered 200 and they all arrived alive and well. They were only one day old and had never seen their mothers, as they had been hatched in incubators, so they had no idea how to get food and even how to eat it. That's when my job began. All 200 chicks were carefully placed in a small heated hen house which had a kerosene-heated brooder with a hood over it to concentrate the heat. For the first few days, I sat with these chicks and taught them how to eat by tapping a finger into their food. They caught on rapidly and eagerly pecked at their mash-filled dishes and found their tasty (to them) morsels. They also learned to drink from their water jars. I really enjoyed this job, even though I was only six when I started. The babies would climb into my lap when they were tired and no longer hungry. I often sat on the floor with a lap full of little yellow balls of fluff. They were all supposed to be White Leghorns, which are yellow when they hatch, but there was one Barred Rock in the batch, which had brownish markings. We named her Jenny, after our nearest neighbor's housekeeper, a Mrs. Flemming. This hen grew to adulthood as a badly spoiled chicken because she was different. We always fed her first because we felt that the others were discriminating against her. She enjoyed her position and grew immensely fat from being overfed.

When the chicks were older and their feathers had grown in, they were transferred to the main hen house, a structure about fifty feet in length, with a wire window for fresh air, bars for roosting, and little boxes arranged in a row for them to lay their eggs into. They usually did this. Mama loved these chickens and felt that they would certainly benefit from individual attention, so whenever she fed them, she would also pet them. They enjoyed this good life and apparently felt loved. Whenever they were outdoors and they saw anyone coming, they happily ran to meet them, squatted directly in front of them, waiting to be petted. You had to know this, or else you could easily trip over them! They were let out of their hen house during the day, so that they could forage for themselves but at night, they had to be rounded up to get back into their enclosure. This was my job. They really wanted to get back in, but their little bird brains screwed them up. This enclosure was surrounded by a six foot chicken wire fence. As I carefully herded them towards the door, each hen stuck her head into one opening in the wire after another until she got to the door, and then immediately rushed past it, looking neither left nor right. And then the whole operation had to start over at the beginning. After I got my dog, it was a lot easier. The dog would stand at the other side of the door to discourage escaping hens from going around again.

We kept the hens for their eggs. Every Monday morning the Egg Man would drive up in his truck and buy the eggs. My Sunday night job was to help my mother clean the eggs with a rag dipped in diluted vinegar and pack them into crates. Later on, when we were in a slightly better financial position, my parents were able to buy their own incubator, which was also heated with kerosene. Getting all this kerosene from the general store must have been quite a chore. Papa had a choice; hitch the horse up to the wagon or take the canoe. Fortunately, the general store in Brookview was right on the river. The kitchen range burned wood, which was in plentiful supply. The river sometimes froze over in the winter, But then we only needed kerosene for the lamps, as farming activities come to a standstill in winter.

My job with the incubating eggs was to candle them. This was one of my favorite jobs! After the eggs had been in the incubator for seven days, I would hold each egg over a flashlight to see if there was a heart beating in it and also if major blood vessels had started growing. It was really thrilling to see life actually beginning! The original Ultra Sound, without pictures. After 14 days, the eggs were filled with chicken embryos and were completely opaque. At 21 days they hatched and we had a new batch of chicks to start the whole process over again.

CHAPTER 6

MY KITTIES

My long-standing affection for cats began on the farm. One day, Papa had pedaled his bicycle back from the general store in Brookview where he had gone to buy staples while I was confined to my bed with a cold. He had brought something else home as well. He came into my room and took an object out of his backpack and put in on my bed. It was a very tiny kitten! And a very hungry one at that. Before I turned seven, I was a very poor eater and drove my poor mother to distraction. My breakfast was still uneaten that morning, so I gave this sweet fluffy little creature a small piece of my unconsumed bun. She ate it eagerly, so I gave her another and another. This was great, my breakfast was being eaten, and not by me. After she finished the bun, I gave her the rest of my milk.

We named her "Mooshie". I just loved her so much. She followed me all around the farm. My very own pet! It turned out shortly thereafter that she wasn't the tiny, young kitten we thought she was. She was just undernourished and small, but a bit more mature than anyone suspected. One evening, just about dusk, a fairly large animal was seen lurking around our house, but it was too dark to make out what it really was. Then little gifts of dead mice began appearing on our porch. Who was bringing them? We soon found out. They were courtship gifts; the large animal was a very handsome gray tomcat with glowing yellow eyes who had taken a fancy to our Mooshie. The inevitable soon happened and Mooshie had a litter of one kitten, no doubt because she was so young and small. We did not know where the Tom had come from. He never said, but liked the setup at our house very much; a nice lady cat friend and regular meals. We called him "Newcomer" and he became a permanent resident. He was never actually invited to come into the house, but that never deterred him. He found that if he pulled at the bottom of the screen door long enough, the hook on the door would eventually bounce off the ring holding it in place, and one final tug would open the door and Newcomer could stroll right in. He was a generous cat and would perform this trick for any of his descendants who also desired entrance to the kitchen, after him of course.

He had another self-taught trick which never failed to impress. If he had managed to sneak into the house at mealtimes, he would sit up and beg, his front paws held demurely in front of him. However, he felt that his efforts certainly deserved to be rewarded, and if they were not, you would quickly find out, because the paws, with claws extended, would give you a good swipe! He was really a different sort of cat. He must have been living on his own for quite a while, so he knew how to fish. He would stand in the river up to his knees on three legs and hold one paw uplifted, ready to bat any unsuspecting minnow which swam too close to him right up on the bank. He would then emerge and enjoy a nice shore dinner. A friend from the city once came to visit and went fishing. He had all the necessary equipment and skills and caught quite a few fish. As he caught them, he tossed them into a bucket of water behind him. When he thought he had enough for a meal, he turned around to count the fish he had. To his astonishment, the bucket was empty! Newcomer had noticed what was going on and had been silently stealing the fish out of the bucket, one by one. The entire cat family had also discovered the great bonanza that Grampa Newcomer did not mind sharing, and were all sitting around the empty bucket, contentedly washing their faces. They were very happy to let someone else do the catching, as long as they got to share. We never saw any of them try to catch their own!

Mama had always loved cats, my father not so much. But he admired skill, both human and feline. So Newcomer rated very highly with him, also certain other cats who were excellent mousers. In the Fall, when the corn shocks have dried, they are knocked over and the dried ears of corn are harvested. Corn shocks are a paradise for mice, and when my father was ready to harvest the corn, he'd call the dog and they would set out for the corn field, followed by a whole tribe of cats. They all knew exactly what was going to happen. As soon as he knocked over the shock, the mice ran out in all directions, pursued by the dog and all the cats. Papa especially admired one named Blackie, who, not surprisingly, was black! He was seen with a mouse under each front paw and one in his mouth, and thus was immobilized. What to do now, this was a real dilemma!

And then there was Peter. He was a really nice cat, but a bit on the lazy side. His favorite spot was my doll's bed. He really relished sleeping in it. He was a big cat, so big that he barely fit, so if there was already a doll in it, she would have to go, be kicked out so Peter could curl up, make himself comfortable and purr himself to sleep. He, too, liked to follow me around. One day I was walking back and forth on the scaffold my father had built out over the river so that he could hang a fish net on it when the herring and shad were running in the spring time. Peter got a bit too close to my feet once, and down he went, into the icy water, as it was still early spring. He gave me a disgusted look and swam back to shore without any difficulty. He climbed out and shook himself and headed for the house. I knew exactly where he would go, and sure enough, there he was, in the doll bed. "Poor, precious, Peter", I said. "Are you OK?" He limply extended a paw and promptly began to purr, but never did he follow me on the scaffold again!

CHAPTER 6.5

DOLL HOUSE

While we were still living in City Island, my father and his friend, Uncle Rudy, who were both unemployed at the time, decided to build me a doll house, and a wonderful doll house it turned out to be. They used an old dynamite box which was probably 36" x 36" and 12" deep. I know it was a dynamite box, because the word "DYNAMITE" could still be read on the back of the box, despite the several coats of white paint that had been applied to it. Uncle Rudy was an electrician and had access to these boxes when he was employed. The house had five rooms and an attic. The attic contained the most interesting feature, the batteries needed to power the electric lights! However, the batteries needed to be replaced frequently, as the lights were constantly being switched on and off. The house also had a fake fireplace in the corner of the living room. This also lit up when the lights were switched on, as there was only one switch. A flashlight bulb had been secured behind crumpled up red and yellow paper which had been stuffed into the fake fireplace. The result was quite realistic. This doll house was an absolute Kid Magnet! They kept coming to the door, wanting to play with it and my mother let them in. I would have been far more selective myself and only would have let in kids who could be relied on not to destroy, break or otherwise wreck havoc on the house and its furnishings. On one occasion, after the hordes had left, Papa said, "Clean up the mess your friends have made." I became highly indignant, "They aren't my friends, I didn't invite them in, so why should I have to clean up after them?" I thought I had a valid point, but my father wouldn't buy this argument from a five-year old, and spanked me! For years I kept after him, rearguing my case, so finally after about twenty years, he finally conceded that I had been right.

I still had the doll house when we moved to Maryland, and the electric lights were still working, which incidently could not be said about the house in which we lived. No electricity there! Once, the neighbors who lived on the other side of the highway came over to visit and brought their three daughters with them. They played with the well-lit doll house which was a great attraction for them, as their own home was also illuminated by kerosene lamps. They were older than I and careful, so there was no breakage problem. When they got tired playing with the lights, they decided to inquire about my education. I had told them I had been in kindergarten, which did not exist in Dorchester County, and that I would not be entering first grade for another six months. Then they asked me if I could count. As I didn't want to stand there and count for them, I said, "No". Big mistake! They immediately decided to teach me. So, instead of just counting to 100 for them, I also had to pretend to learn. They were quite impressed with the speed at which I learned. But I found out at a very early age that my parents were right about lying. Don't do it! They never mentioned that falsehoods really don't save any time at all!

CHAPTER 7

MERRY CHRISTMAS

What should have been our first Christmas in Maryland was actually celebrated by Mama and me in New York. My sister, Lori, who was sixteen years older than I, had just given birth to her first baby, little Elinore, on Dec. 2, 1931. Mama had come up to help her, and I, of course came along and was obliged to bring with me an incredible amount of homework assigned by my teacher, Mrs. Rodgers. "Don't worry about Margaret, Mrs. Wentzel," Mrs. Rodgers said. "The homework I have assigned will be easy for her, and she will have it finished in no time at all." Sure, easy for her to say!

We arrived a day before Lori and Elinore were to come home from the hospital so that Mama could straighten up the apartment in which my brother-in-law, Adolf and the dog, Trixie had been leading carefree lives for two weeks. We had come up on the train to Penn Station and then took the subway to Ridgewood, which is located on the Brooklyn-Queens border, in New York City. It must have been quite an accomplishment for my mother who had never been good with subways. At six years of age, I was no help at all. In later years, when we were back living in New York City, Mama only shopped at Bloomingdales, because it was so easy to get to from Astoria or Elmhurst, where we eventually lived, on the BMT subway. It was the first stop after the tunnel.

When Lori and the baby came home, I was sort of disappointed. I had no idea what to expect, never having been around babies that small before. When we first got the news, our neighbor, Mr. Palisada, said to me, "You're an aunt now, isn't that wonderful?" I was puzzled.

My own aunts, my mother's four older sisters, all lived in Germany. I would only have had dim memories of them if they had not written letters to me that my mother read aloud, and sent little trinkets. When I was born, they all made a big fuss over me, because they were older and their kids were all in their late teens or in their early twenties, some with children of their own. So, to me aunts were old ladies. How did I fit into this category? I was only six years old! I thought perhaps I could play with the baby, but when I saw her, I knew that was not an option, she looked so small, even though she was really a big baby, but I didn't know that! I didn't expect her to be so tiny. And, it turned out, she slept all day and cried all night. It would have been hard to establish any sort of relationship with her. Meanwhile, Mama kept reminding me about my undone homework.

My sister had a number of friends who had little girls I could play with. One of them was named Myrtle and we spent a lot of time together. One afternoon, Myrtle and I wrote letters to Santa Claus, detailing the gifts we would like to receive. The following morning I got up early and was wandering aimlessly around the living room when I received quite a shock. I discovered Myrtle's letter to Santa torn into little pieces and tossed into an ashtray. What could be the meaning of this? Was Myrtle's mother so angry with her for some reason that she didn't want her to get any presents? Or maybe there was no Santa to send those letters to? Nah, couldn't be, even though I had heard rumors! As I stood there debating with myself what to do about this situation, I came to the conclusion that no action at all would be the best course of action. So I said nothing to anybody, especially not Myrtle. Anyway it wasn't MY letter in the ashtray. Of course not! My mother saved everything. Years later, she came across this letter and showed it to me. We had to laugh, not only did it list the gifts I wanted, I also wanted to make sure that Santa knew that it was Trixie, the dog who had chewed up the box of spaghetti, not me. Evidently I didn't want any demerits for misbehavior! It did probably put me on the snitch list though.

Christmas came and went and many gifts were received, including those that were tucked into my slipper that was left on the window sill every night from Advent to the day before Christmas Eve. This is an old German custom, observed in Holland and the Scandanavian countries as well. Naturally, with all these celebrations, my homework remained undone, even though my mother was constantly reminding me to do it!

After New Year's Day, Mama and I were scheduled to go back home to Maryland. For New Year's Eve, my sister and her husband had a few friends over to celebrate. I remember the noisemakers, colorful little horns, whistles and rattles. I ran around the apartment, blowing and rattling more than anyone. How could the baby have slept through all this racket? It had been a very satisfactory New Year's Party for me. I did not last until midnight, in spite of being told that I was allowed to. I was asleep by 10:30!

Well, another day, another year, 1932. I could not put off doing my homework any longer, as we would be returning home in less than a week. So, I sat down and completed it. My mother was pleased. "At last", she said. "If you had done it as soon as we got here, we would not have had all this wrangling and you could have enjoyed your visit here much more." Did not matter to me any more. It was finally finished and could be handed in to my teacher with pride and the Sword of Damocles had been removed from above my head! As a special reward I was allowed to hold the baby. This had not happened before. She weighed more than eight pounds and no way would a six-year old like me be allowed to pick her up. So I sat on my sister's bed and she put the baby on my lap. This was a big thrill, another step in the growing-up process! Elinore was really kind of cute, especially as she wasn't crying. I thought that there was hope for this child yet.

For Christmas, one of my gifts had been two little doll chairs which were pink. They were really nice and my dolls sat around in them all day and goofed off. They must have been really comfortable. The day of departure came and we traveled back to Papa and the farm. There was a surprise waiting for me. Unbelievably, Santa Claus had delivered a pink table to match the chairs to the house in Maryland! I was truly amazed. I guess that would put to rest all those rumors about the non-existence of Santa! Later, on my birthday in April, I received a tiny tablecloth for this table which I was supposed to embroider. I did finish it, but I think it took a few years, speed was never my thing. I had acquired a few more pieces of furniture for my dolls, a little dresser with three drawers that opened and shut, and a bed, which Peter, the cat fancied so much. These were painted green.

When I was about eight, my father was busy every night after supper working on a wooden contraption that I could not figure out. In answer to my questions, he said, "It's something for the chickens", but he did not elaborate. This got me thinking, "Is he going to build one of these things for each of the chickens?" It would surely take him longer than forever, seeing how long it was taking him to make only one. I did not find out until Christmas Eve what it was that he was actually doing. At that time, before kitchen counters and hanging cabinets, a popular piece of kitchen furniture was a free-standing cabinet that had storage space below for pots and pans, a work area above that, and enclosed space for food staples directly above this work area. On one side there was a built-in flour sifter. In our area it was called a Hoover Cabinet, although I have since heard it referred to as a Hoosier Cabinet. I do not know which name is correct. Well, it turned out that the mysterious chicken thingy was really a miniature Hoover Cabinet, which I received that Christmas. Santa, of course, had long since departed for fantasy land. It was just so cute, Papa spared no details, he had fashioned tiny metal drawer pulls and knobs. The only thing he never got to make was the flour sifter. So the dolls didn't get baked goods!

Christmas was a pretty big deal for me. First we had to go into the woods to pick out a tree. Not as easy as it sounds, even though the woods are full of trees, Most people used cedar trees, which didn't look bad and had a nice smell, but it was not the smell of spruce and fir which symbolized Christmas for us. We settled on a short-leaf pine instead. Mama loved the smell and after a long search a suitable one could usually be found. Then it was taken home and Papa went to work on it so that it would be perfect, boring holes in the trunk to insert branches where they were missing and trimming the others to conform. Then came the tricky part. We used candles to light it. My parents worked on this part. There were twelve candle holders, and even though the candles sat on a ball joint to hold the candles straight, placement was everything. Mama loved the candles. Even after we moved back to N.Y. we always had the dozen candles on the tree. It was an awe-inspiring sight. She would never even consider electric lights! Our only fire prevention precaution was-NOBODY MOVE! We could sing Christmas Carols and guess which candle would be the last to go out, but NOBODY MOVE! Even after my sister's twins were born, it was still the same story, NOBODY MOVE!

After the candle holders were in place and candles inserted to make sure they would stand straight when they were lit, it was my turn to hang the ornaments. We had a lot of them, some dating back to when my sister was eight, in 1916, when Mama had made a special tree for her. My mother was working as a nurse in an army hospital at the time and wasn't able to come home to Lori very often. Therefore my sister stayed with one relative after another. Luckily my mother had four sisters!

CHAPTER 8

DOG DAYS

When we lived on the farm in Maryland, our nearest neighbors were the Beabouts. Mrs. B, her husband Oscar and her brother, Andy. It was about a 45 minute walk through the woods to get to their farm from ours. They had a much bigger and a much more prosperous farm than ours, and had a lot more livestock than my parents. They had a large bull, which was somewhat intimidating, so I needed no warnings to stay away from him. He was big and scary! They owned a tom turkey, who was also threatening in his own way. And then there were the dogs. Behind their house there was a chain link enclosure with barbed wire strung along the top. In this enclosure were three totally ferocious and untamed dogs. They barked and growled whenever anyone came near the fence. Mr. and Mrs. B kept them as their security system. Those dogs had quite a reputation in the neighborhood, so no one would even think of committing any sort of mischief on the B's property. In retrospect, I realize that those dogs were more to be pitied than feared. They didn't even live a dog's life! There were lots of other animals as well; chickens, pigs, cows and calves, female turkeys. It was a lively place.

The father of the ferocious dogs was called Fruple and Mrs. B insisted that he was part wolf. He looked and acted like a nice friendly shepherd dog. That dog loved me. I guess no one else paid much attention to him or gave him much affection. Therefore, we were the best of friends. Money was scarce in 1932, so my mother was very happy to get a job cooking and cleaning for Mrs. B, who preferred working in the fields, harder probably than most men. Mama worked there five days a week for the fabulous sum of $10 a month! But it helped, it was money my parents didn't have before.

Anyway, to get back to the dogs. I stayed on the school bus and got off at Beabout's place, so that I could walk home with my mother when she was finished with her work, eliminating the necessity of having some one come to pick me up. Fruple knew exactly when the bus was due to arrive and would be sitting by the mailbox, wagging his tail, waiting for his favorite person to arrive. The other kids on the bus, knowing the reputation of the B's dogs, were flabbergasted to see me playing with one of them. My reputation was greatly enhanced! We had great times together. I would check out the ditch that ran alongside the highway to see how the tadpoles were coming along. First the legs would appear and grow longer and longer, while the tail became shorter and shorter until it was completely absorbed into the body. One day there would be a chorus of frogs sitting on the bank and there would be no tadpoles left swimming in the water. Fruple always enjoyed a good game of stick toss and we played it a lot. Toys for dogs? Unheard of in those days. Kids might be lucky enough to get a toy sometimes, but a dog? Come on!

There were also two house dogs, dogs permitted indoors, Fruple was not. They had the rather sickenly sweet names of Sugar Plum and Baby Girl. Baby Girl was Fruple's daughter. Sugar Plum looked vaguely like a collie. Mrs. B said he was a show dog. Nobody ever believed that. Actually she may have said he was a chow dog, but my parents, with their accents, might have misunderstood her. In any case, he wasn't exactly a chow either, perhaps he might have been about 1/64th chow! Baby Girl was expecting puppies. Mrs. B. promised me that I could have one. When Baby Girl delivered, there was my puppy! The only one, she had only one puppy, and it was mine! When she was old enough to be taken home, we named her Dina, short for Diana, Goddess of the hunt. Exactly why I don't know. Certainly Papa didn't plan to go hunting. Mrs. B insisted that the proper way to raise a dog was to tie it up in the yard, so that's what my father did, very reluctantly. We all felt sorry for her and I spent a lot of time playing with her in the yard. Papa had tied her with a nice long rope, but we felt that the dog should come into the house with us. It was heart-breaking for me to see my puppy put her front paws around one of my ankles to keep me from leaving her. When the weather started to turn cold in the fall, Mama said, "Enough is enough, the dog is coming into the house with us!" And so, in she came. She was a wonderful dog, automatically housebroken and just fit into the house as if she had always been living there. Didn't need any kind of training at all, everything just came naturally to her. As for being a watchdog, it was just instinctive. One only had to ask, "Is something the matter?" and she would bark long and loud. Upon hearing "OK", she would stop in mid-bark.

Dina was my constant companion, going everywhere I did. My mother no longer had to be nervous when I went wandering off in the woods or playing at the river's edge at low tide. Mama had given me an old sugar sack and I put every lovely pebble I found into it, and I found plenty. The sack got pretty heavy. Of course, they were ever so much prettier when they were wet, but as I had neither the skill or the equipment to polish them, they had to be kept wet so they would look nice and shiny when they were displayed.

Further away from the house, on the sandy road, there was a high sand bluff above the river. This was unusual, the rest of the farm was very flat, maybe only a few feet above sea level. This sand bluff was my chief source of Indian arrow heads and pottery shards. I wasn't very impressed with the shards. I wanted to find a complete pot, plate or whatever, intact, which never happened. Even the arrowheads were far from being prime specimens. Papa said the Marshyhope Indians must have had a school for apprentice arrow head chippers on this bluff and all I was finding were the rejects!

CHAPTER 9

A WALK ON THE WILD SIDE

Our house was set back from the highway approximately at the end of one or one and a half miles of woodland. Our property did not extend that far, but we had the right of way on the dirt roads that led to the paved road along which the school bus traveled. This bus was not only for the children going to Eldorado Grammar School, but also when these younger kids were discharged at their destination, the bus continued on to Hurlock, where the older kids attended high school. One of my parents always accompanied me on these walks to get to the bus, it was usually my mother. Nothing untoward ever happened there, but Mama was taking no chances! Despite my protests that I was perfectly capable of walking by myself, she absolutely would not hear of it. On these jaunts, there were always animals who wanted to come along. After I got Dina, my dog, it seemed perfectly natural that she would accompany us. After all, that's what dogs are expected to do. Before that, though, there were others. We had kittens who considered this a wonderful treat, so different from their everyday lives. Mama regarded this cat entourage as completely unnecessary. It was mostly the younger cats, the teenagers, who just had to come, but they tired of the trip long before Mama got back home. So she was compelled to carry them the rest of the way. One morning there were two of them following us at a distance, and my mother said," We are going to teach those cats a lesson." As soon as we were out of sight due to bend in the road, she said, "Quick, behind those big trees, we'll hide from them, and when they no longer see us, they'll turn around and just go back home." Soon they proudly marched past us, heads and tails held high, keeping in perfect step with each other, looking neither left nor right. It didn't take them long to notice that they were no longer following anyone. They turned around in total disarray and started back home, wailing and crying inconsolably. It was such a heart-breaking scene, we had to relent and forget about the lesson. We picked both of them up and comforted them until they started purring. I carried one and Mama carried the other up to the highway. When the bus came, I handed my kitten to my mother, who put it into her all-purpose apron pocket, and I boarded the bus. Well, so much for teaching cats!

We had also acquired a lamb, which was called Nanny. My parents probably thought a sheep was just a sheep. You raise them to a certain size, and then lamb chops and legs of lamb. However, no one ever thought to factor in the pet thing. Pets should never become food. They must each be kept on their own separate level. The purpose of pigs and chickens was always clear to me, so I never became emotionally attached to them. But Nanny had no flock of other sheep to hang out with so she became a very strong-minded individual, in no way a herd animal. She, too, like walking to the school bus, and was forever finding a way to escape from the barn to join us. One morning was very different. It was raining and Mama and I were walking with opened umbrellas. Nanny, as always, found a way out of the barn and was happily bleating to announce her presence, when she spotted the umbrellas. This was all new to her and she did not like it at all! She did a quick about-face and ran back into the barn for sanctuary from these very strange objects.

Most of the time, the weather was nice and Nanny came along with us. Mama did not trust her to stay off the highway, so she used her all-purpose apron as a lamb leash. Once a neighbor offered her a ride back home before he noticed the livestock accompanying her, then promptly rescinded his offer! When we had to leave the farm for an hour or two, Nanny was confined to an empty henhouse. This was fine as long as no one was home. She was perfectly contented, but the moment she heard voices, she would jump through the window, which was covered by some kind of translucent fabric, just like a trained circus animal jumping through a paper hoop, then stand there, waiting for a round of applause

The inevitable sad ending finally happened. One day I saw a sheep carcass hanging in the barn. I cried and lamented, "That's Nanny, why did you have to kill her?" My parents insisted that they had traded Nanny for the carcass of another sheep. I never believed it and have always avoided eating lamb.

CHAPTER 10

PLANTS AND FLOWERS

Mama always had a great love for plants and flowers. There had always been plants in our home, many that even bloomed and were really gorgeous. She had grown up in a land where it was quite commonplace to bring a bouquet of flowers to someone you were visiting, it did not require a special occasion. When we moved to the farm in Maryland, there was plenty of room for all kinds of decorative plants outdoors and therefore it was unnecessary to bring them indoors. Conditions were good and they grew well, but the time to care for them was limited. There was always so much work that needed to be done that there was little time for luxuries like raising flowers. But the world would be such a dreary place if we could not indulge ourselves to an occasional treat of something beautiful.

That was my mother's thinking, and actually my father agreed with her. She said, "Ernst, please find the time to move that large lilac bush. It has been in that shady location for two years and has never bloomed. It needs a sunnier spot." He moved it to a spot where the two dirt roads converged that was always sunny. These roads surrounded an oval area, which had a number of nice maple trees, a very large poplar and some haphazardly planted shrubs. This was our front yard. There were also a few apple trees, which flowered nicely, but whose apples never stayed on the trees. Mama expected the lilacs to flower, and so they did, profusely. Every year thereafter, the bush was loaded with blossoms. There were plenty to be picked and brought into the house, which was then filled with their wonderful aroma. We also had a wisteria bush which grew and grew, twining itself around the apple trees and producing an incredible number of flowers. This bush was apparently very happy where it was and did not require transplanting. They have bracts of very attractive purple flowers which hang down in bunches. These were also picked and inserted into vases.

The school sponsored a 4 H Club which I was not very fond of because it discriminated against children from families who were poorer than we were and could not afford the minimal cost of supplies. They were therefore compelled to do the hated busy work, while the rest of us learned to cook, sew and do other projects. The boys were taught to do farm things. One of the girls' projects was to create a flower basket out of a shoe box. I covered my shoe box with crepe paper I had saved from gifts given me by visitors from New York, probably my sister. Nothing potentially useful was ever thrown away. After all these years, I am still trying to break this habit! I had filled the basket with bracts of wisteria flowers. It was very effective and looked nice until the flowers started to wilt. These baskets were to be given to senior citizens in an Old Folks' Home. I hope they lasted long enough to get to their recipient!

We always had plenty of flowers to cut. The apple and peach trees in back of the house always had many flowers, and it was OK to pick generously, as they never produced edible fruit. The little green fruit always fell off before it ripened. Not so the pear trees, they always bore lots and lots of delicious fruit, so those flowers were not for picking! Anyway, they were plain white, and the pink peach flowers and the pink and white apple blossoms were much prettier.

One incident remains indelibly in my mind. One morning, on one of our twice daily walks through the woods to get to and from the school bus that came down Route 313, my mother and I came upon a breath-taking sight. There popped out of the ground, under the tall loblolly pines, through the pine sheds underneath them, stood the most incredibly beautiful flower we had ever seen! It was a luminous pink puff, about three inches long, emerging from a stem about a foot high. We could hardly believe our eyes, it seemed almost mystical to see something so gorgeous in such dark, foreboding, gloomy surroundings. We looked for it twice a day, each time we passed by and could not stop marveling that this could happen. It lasted for several weeks before it dried up. We never saw another like it anywhere in the woods. Later on, when we were able to access botanical books, we were able to look it up and discovered that it was a pink lady slipper, a ground orchid.

CHAPTER 11

HUNTING?

Late autumn weather brought with it an odd form of entertainment to the Delmarva Peninsula. By this time the crops had been safely harvested, the hay had been carefully stored in hay stacks, to insure that that cows and horses would have enough food to last the winter, as purchasing it from an outsource would be prohibitively expensive. To make certain that the hay would not spoil, it had to be absolutely dry before it could be arranged around a pole in such a fashion that the outer layers formed a thatched coating to keep the inner layers dry and protected from rain and snow. If this were not done exactly right and the inside of the stack was even slightly damp, a tremendous amount of heat could build up and the stack might explode into flames caused by spontaneous combustion, destroying that stack and the adjacent ones as well. This would leave the farmer without winter food for his livestock. Nothing was worse than rain on harvest day. If it did rain, the whole drying process had to be done all over again. The quality of the hay did not improve by redrying it. Today, it is done differently. I never see hay stacks anymore. It is rolled up instead.

The corn had been shucked, the ears removed and safely stored in the corn crib. Some of the green corn stalks had been cut during the summer, when it was still fresh, and stored in silos, where a sort of fermentation process took place, making the corn plants easier for the cows to digest and maybe tastier. The cows never said, but seemed to enjoy them.

With less work, the farmers had some spare time on their hands, so at night they mounted their horses, called their dogs and went fox hunting, whooping and hollering through the woods. The racket they made could be heard in the next county for sure. This all but guaranteed that any fox had plenty of warning and time to escape. Not that I think they actually wished the foxes any harm. They just liked to cut loose! As they only hunted at night and kept up the noise for hours on end, accompanied by the barking, yelping and howling of the excited hounds, it was hard to get much sleep! I say foxes, although I'm not at all sure that there was more than one. Certainly there weren't many. In six years of walking through the woods, Mama and I only caught a quick glimpse of one, shyly peeking around a tree behind us. When he saw that he had been observed, he melted back into the forest.

As we were speaking of hunting, my father and our friend Alex were out in the woods one day, marking dead trees that needed taking out, when they encountered a most unusual sight. The small brook that was the western boundary of our property must have overflowed during a heavy storm and had left a fairly large puddle when the rest of the flood receded. In this puddle was a large pike that barely fit. There was no way this fish could get back into the brook and follow it down into the river. The puddle was getting smaller every day, as it was drying up. Papa sent Alex back to the house, saying, "Go ask Grete to give you my gun. This could make us a nice fish dinner." Alex, a recent immigrant from the German state of Saxony, spoke a very fractured English and with a strong dialect when he spoke German, especially when he got excited. Which he was now. My mother understood the part about the gun, but the rest of the story was incomprehensible to her. Why would her husband even think about wanting to shoot a deer, especially since there weren't known to be any in that part of the country? After a good deal of effort, she did get the story straight. Alex was saying "Hecht" which is pike in German, but with his strong dialect, it sounded like "Hirsch" which is deer, to my mother. Still puzzled about the fish story, she reluctantly handed him the shot gun and he took off, running back into the woods. The climax to this story came when the fish was gutted and an undigested mole was discovered in its stomach! That's all Mama had to see. "We are not eating that fish, get rid of it now!" She was adamant, besides being a revolting sight, my mother had an almost pathological aversion to rodents. The pike had to go. Alex not wanting to waste food, took it home to his sister, Probably leaving out the part of the story involving the mole!

If it seems that we spent a lot of time in the woods, it's because we did. We were surrounded by trees, weren't able to get anywhere without going through the woods, except by way of the river. This forest consisted mostly of pine trees, long and short needled varieties. These were interspersed with oaks, maples and cedars. Some of which turned to brilliant shades of yellow, red, and orange in the colder autumn weather. The dead trees were fuel for the kitchen range and the Franklin stove in the living room. This room was only used on special occasions, Christmas or company. The dead needles from the long leaf pines, called pine sheds were used as bedding for the cows and horses instead of straw. This was convenient and cheap, available for just for the picking up! I accompanied Papa many times when he took the horse and wagon to pick up pine sheds.

The horse's name was Julie and she was a really smart horse. Papa use her mostly to pull the plow, but sometimes she was hitched up to the wagon when larger items had to be transported. He always maintained that she must have at one time been used to pull a delivery wagon by her previous owner. She was a very fast horse, but she certainly looked nothing like a race horse. Julie moved so fast that my father was forced to run, just to keep up with her. He lost forty pounds the first year! She also had an annoying habit of appearing at the front porch very early in the morning, neighing to be fed. That horse had a wonderful appetite! Warm nights she spent in a corral built of logs piled on top of each other, only with wider spaces between them. Papa could not figure it out. How did she escape every morning? He kept piling on more logs to make the corral higher, eventually it got to be about six feet high. Despite this ever increasing height, Julie showed up faithfully at first light, neighing to be fed, as usual. My father said, "How can she possibly jump so high? Much younger, steeplechase ponies don't jump that high." He determined to see this for himself, so very early one morning, he got up in the dark and hid next to the barn. As soon as it got slightly lighter, the mystery was solved. Julie got down on her knees and crawled under the bottom log of the corral, in order to arrive at the front porch just at sunrise, and neigh for her breakfast! She had probably not even noticed that the logs were getting higher and higher every day.

CHAPTER 12

THE HURRICANE

Sometime during the summer of 1933, we had a hurricane come through our area, the Eastern Shore. I know the year because my little niece, Elinore, was staying with us for the summer. She was able to walk and had started talking in sentences. Well, two word sentences. I estimate her age at about 18 months, which would have been 1933, as she was born in December. 1931. Elinore's favorite sentence was, "Bunny apple", which meant that she wanted to feed the rabbits with the little green apples that fell off the trees. They had never ripened and we had pretty much given up that they ever would, the same could be said for the peach trees, but they did have lovely, fragrant flowers every spring. The fruit that these trees produced wasn't fit for anything except feeding the bunnies. They seemed to enjoy them. Nice change from grass, I suppose. The only productive fruit trees we had were the pears. They were very tall, as nobody had ever pruned them and were loaded with pears every year. We had fresh pears, preserved pears, pear jam, pear jelly, pear pies, pear tarts and pear pudding. We had plenty of pears!

But, back to the hurricane. We had no idea that one was forming in the Atlantic, offshore. We received no warning because we had no radio. I don't think battery operated radios even existed in those days, not that we would have ever possessed such a luxury item, anyhow. Perhaps warnings weren't even issued then. Two years later, the dreadful 1935 Labor Day hurricane struck the Florida Keys without official warning. Some ships captains had reported the approach of a severe storm, but that was about all. The some four hundred war veterans who had been working on the Overseas Railroad, were left waiting on the train for orders to come through for the train to be moved to the mainland. The order to move the train never came, and most of the veterans drowned, as did many of the local residents. There is a monument in Islamorada honoring these victims, many of whom were never identified and are buried beneath the monument.

We had no idea that there was a storm coming. The day had been sunny, warm and pleasant, a typical summer day for us. Towards nightfall, the wind had started picking up and became quite strong. Later the rain started to fall and the wind became stronger and stronger. My father became concerned about a large poplar tree that was growing about a dozen feet away from the front of the house. It had an enormous trunk, and was at least ten feet in circumference, and was accordingly, quite high. Large as it was, that tree started to sway. Papa was afraid that it might fall on the house, so he attached guy wires and chains to it. In retrospect, I can't imagine that anything like that, hurriedly rigged up in the dark could really be expected to hold up this giant tree, but we were fortunate, the winds shifted in the night. This was possibly the eye wall passing over us, but we knew nothing of such things. All we knew was that the tree held up and we were really grateful. What we didn't know until daylight revealed it the next morning, was that an equally large poplar tree on the other side of the house had fallen, luckily away from the house and down the embankment towards the river. That was a night we were all glad was over. There were no worries about losing electrical power. That thought never occurred to us as we had been already living without it for two years.

Everything seemed fine, but then Mama looked out at the fields and exclaimed," Why are the pigs rooting around in the peanut field? How did they get out?" Well, the pigs were having a picnic, enjoying peanuts as they munched away. Papa always felt that pigs were very much maligned as being dirty animals, wallowing in the mud when all they really wanted to do is keep cool. He found a novel solution to the problem; extend their pen down the hill into the river, where they could bathe when the tide came in to their heart's content and keep nice and cool. They deserved humane treatment throughout their lives, even though their lives would be short and eventually they would be eaten. This had always worked well until the storm brought an abnormally high tide during the night and the water came up over the top of the pen. The pigs saw an opportunity to supplement their diet and swam over the top to go exploring. That's when they found the peanut field, pig paradise! It wasn't difficult to get them to go back to their pen. My father took their food bucket and banged on it with a stick-the time honored dinner bell for pigs, and they promptly came home. To an empty bucket, no sense letting them make pigs of themselves!

There had been no real damage from the storm. All of the buildings were still standing, even though the lower-lying fields were under water. When the tide went out, it all drained away. It wasn't salt water, as the salt doesn't come up as far the tides, so there was no harm done. Everything dried as if it had just been a very heavy rain. Elinore and I went outside and fed the bunnies with apples once again.

CHAPTER 13

WHAT'S IN A NAME?

Why did the original settlers name the town Eldorado [spelled as one word]? There is no obvious reason at all. I simply cannot believe that anyone had ever expected to find gold there. The terrain is just not supportive of that idea. It is located in what is called the Delmarva Peninsula. This name is derived from the three states that comprise this peninsula, the entire state of Delaware, the eastern shore of Maryland, and the Cape Charles section of Virginia. Eons ago, it might have been formed by glaciers which ripped out the Chesapeake Bay, or perhaps it was the remains of a delta deposited by the Delaware River in some long ago era. In any case, the likelihood of finding gold in the loose sandy soil was non-existent. So why then Eldorado? And why a misspelled Spanish name? There were probably no Spaniards within a hundred mile radius of the town. Perhaps it was a phonetic version of an Indian name? No one seems to know.

It was a very small town, with perhaps forty or so inhabitants. Even today, the 2010 census showed that there were sixty people living there. However, it does seem to be growing, in 2000, there were only 49. So I guess that is progress! My school was located on State Road 313, on the outskirts of town, just before Route 313 turned to go to Brookview. There was a filling station [known as a gas station today] on each of the corners. Each filling station was also a small general store. The one closest to the school was the most popular, at least to me and my friends. They carried many varieties of penny candy. A careful child like me could stretch the quarter she received as an allowance every two weeks to last the whole ten school days in those two weeks. Two cents' worth of candy every day and a nickel left over to save for Christmas and birthday gifts for my parents, sister and niece. Nobody gave or received expensive gifts! I remember one Christmas when I was old enough to be allowed to pick out gifts for the whole family from the Sears, Roebuck catalog by myself. Of course they had to be ordered by mail, so I told my mother not to look to see what I had ordered for her, which was a set of four stoneware bowls for fifty cents and a donut cutter for a dime. I don't remember what I ordered for anyone else.

The rest of the town of Eldorado consisted of three churches and a scattering of homes along Route 313. When I say there was no gold mined there, that was true, but once I did find gold while poking around in the mud with a stick on the riverbank. It was a massive gold wedding ring, with no engraving on it to supply a clue as to whom it might have belonged, just a 14 K stamp. My parents were thrilled as it was quite heavy. It was sent to New York to a dentist friend who paid us ten dollars for it, a substantial amount in those days. My father said, "Anytime you have nothing better to do, go poke around in the mud for a bit!"

CHAPTER 14

THE BOAT

I had always wanted a little toy boat, nothing fancy, just a tiny sailboat that could be sailed or pulled along with an attached piece of string. The river was right there, it would have been so handy. I kept nagging my father, "Please make me a little boat, Papa. I would love to have a tiny little sailboat that could be sailed on the river". My father was a very busy man, farming took up all his time in the summer, from sunup to sundown, so he certainly had no time to make me a toy. It would have been different in the winter when there was less daylight and less work for him. However, as I was only a kid, it never occurred to me to ask him to make a boat for me then, as I wouldn't be able to use it. During the winter months, the river frequently froze over, as the weather during the thirties was extremely cold. Ice skates would have been nice then, but no way would I ever get ice skates! One Christmas I received short skis that were about twelve inches long so that I could slide around on the snow and stay away from the ever-so-tempting ice on the river. It almost worked. I slid around on these truncated skis looking for hills, but of course, there were none to be found. It was not very exciting, I soon got bored. One day, looking at all that ice on what I considered a solidly frozen river was just too much, I had to test it. It looked fine to me! Somehow, with the sixth sense that Parents have, I was discovered and all my protests that the ice was nice and solid availed me nothing. I was to stay off the ice and that was that!

It does seem a bit strange that my parents were so terrified of my being on the ice and seemed to have no qualms about my swimming by myself in the river during the summer. I do suppose that ice is bit more dangerous, but once when I was about eight years old, I was swimming alone and found that my feet no longer could touch the bottom. After a second or two of panic, I said to myself, "If you can swim when your feet reach bottom, what has changed when you no longer can?" The water kept you afloat before and will continue to do so." So it did and from then on, I was able to swim in deep water, without giving it a second thought!

My father sort of relented and agreed that it would be nice for me to have a small boat as I was in or near the river so much of the time. He took a log off the wood pile, cut one end to a point, and hammered a nail into the front. With the addition of a piece of string tied to the nail, it became a boat, suitable for pulling through the water. It was better than nothing!

Many years later, when I was already married and had long forgotten the boat, my father remembered. He had recently retired and was looking for an interesting hobby. That's when he remembered the boat, and set about to build a far more fabulous model boat than I could ever have imagined. This was definitely NOT a toy, not to be played with and certainly not gotten wet. He did not use a kit, but instead built the whole thing from scratch. The hull had ribs attached to a keel and the external planks were attached one by one, just as a real boat would have been constructed. It was a marvelous miniature eighteenth-century frigate. The three masts had the proper rigging, with the yard arms attached. He had purchased books on the subject to get every detail absolutely correct. He had apprenticed as a cabin boy when he was fourteen, with an eye to becoming a Captain eventually, but found that the voyage around Cape Horn in a four-masted frigate was really not for him. All of his fingers were frost-bitten. The food was terrible as well. Most of it had been on board since the ship had left Hamburg. Mostly, it was Hardtack. I suppose that fresh food was taken on board when the ship was in port, but that probably did not happen often. The reason sailing vessels were still in use at the beginning of the twentieth century was economic. No fuel was required, the wind would hopefully take the ship to its destinations. The cargo certainly would not spoil on a long journey. It was guano, bird droppings that had been accumulating for thousands of years on the islands off the west coast of South America.

It was used for fertilizer and other chemicals. It could not have smelled very good, either!

In spite of this, Papa retained his love for ships, hence the model. As he had gone on to become a jeweler, he was extremely competent in working with metals He turned 26 tiny canons out of brass on a very small lathe, and made an anchor out of German silver, as well as a pierced silver lantern and a bowsprit figurehead of carved wooden lion wearing a crown. The model had six stairways leading to the upper decks, which each had curving ebony handrail and tiny pierced wooden hatches on deck. The wheel was over the rudder and there was a capstan forward. This is a horizontal wheel used to pull up the anchor. This a popular movie scene in movies using sailing vessels, which uses a half dozen sailors turning it to pull up the anchor.

Papa got so caught up in making ship models that he made four more of these exquisite models; two smaller frigates, a Viking longboat, and a Chinese junk.

CHAPTER 15

EXPEDIENCY

S urviving the Great Depression required a lot of ingenuity and improvisation on the part of my parents. Farm life was totally new to them, especially to my mother, who had spent her whole life living in a city. They had very little money and had to stretch that as far as humanly possible. My father received a very small pension from the German government, as he was a war veteran who had been severely wounded twice during the First World War, the war that was to have been the war to end all wars! It was indeed a very small pension, $18 a year. To preserve this incredible pension, my parents could not become American citizens. It seems laughable by today's standards, but that $18 was very important to our survival. It paid for the yearly real estate taxes on the farm.

It was only after the Second World War that we could apply for American citizenship. Throughout the war we were "enemy aliens" and were supposed to carry with us at all times a little pink booklet for identification. However, we considered ourselves fortunate and did not complain. We felt so lucky to be living in the U.S.A. Carrying the little booklets was certainly not a big deal. We were so much better off than the Japanese on the West Coast, who, through no fault of their own, just because of an accident of birth, even though they were United States citizens, either by naturalization or birth, were relieved of their property and put into concentration camps for the duration of the war. Just recently, I believe, the survivors were compensated very minimally by the U.S. Government.

Our citizenship process went well, except that I was terribly offended by the questions the examiner asked me. "Are you married?" he asked. "No", I said. "Ever been married?" "No", "Any kids?" I was shocked that anyone would think to ask such a question! My sister, on the other hand, had memorized the entire booklet outlining the probable questions that could be asked at her hearing. She had answered correctly why we celebrate the Fourth of July, but certainly did not stop there. She went on to give a not-so-brief outline of the Revolutionary War, the first and the second Continental Congresses, and would have continued to recite every bit of that booklet, which she had so thoroughly memorized, but the judge said, "Enough, I know that you know all the answers. Please stop now, I have a lot more applicants".

Years before, on the farm, my father thought that both the sandy soil and the hot summer weather would be ideal for raising tomatoes. And so it was. On the hottest, muggiest day of the year we transplanted the tomatoes. The plants had been started as seeds in a sheltered location, and when they grew to the proper size, were dug up and the transplanting process began. My father went first, digging a hole for the young plants. Mama followed him with the plants, setting one into each hole and tamping it down with her foot. I was at the end of this walking assembly line, watering the plants. It was a sweaty, dirty, mosquito-ridden job. Most years, the tomatoes grew well. Bugs took their quota, but mostly we got a nice crop. However, everyone else in the area also had a nice crop. Often after loading many bushels of tomatoes which all three of us had picked, on the wagon and hitching up the horse and driving all the way to Brookview to the Phillips Tomato Soup Factory, Papa found that they already had a glut of tomatoes and rejected ours. He then had to drive back home with an unsold crop. Mama canned as much as possible and the rest were fed to the pigs. This did not bring in any cash. Some other solution had to be found. That's when we got more chickens and another cow.

On the farm we didn't have a car for many years. It wasn't that great an inconvenience because my folks had never owned a car in their lives, so of course, they didn't really miss it. My dad used his bicycle to pedal to the general store in either Eldorado or Brookview if he did not have a lot to purchase. I f he were taking produce or other large bulky items, he would have to use the horse and wagon. He could also use the canoe to get to Brookview, as it was situated right on the river and he could tie up by the store. This was the same river that flowed right past our house. If I were home from school, I went with him. It was a lovely ride. There were only one or two houses visible from the water, but the scenery was superb. Trees grew right up to the Marshyhope Creek and gracefully dipped their branches into the water. There were many weeping willows and other trees that broke out in catkins in the Spring. They aren't quite as impressive as pussy willow catkins, but they still produced myriads of colors when they started opening up. The young maple leaves were a lovely shade of red when they first appeared, then they turned a translucent chartreuse before they settled for their summertime green. In the fall, of course, they changed to orange and red, due to the absence of chlorophyll, and then to their final brown, and drifted gracefully down into the water and on to the ground. There was also a tulip tree on this stretch of our land that was immediately adjacent to the water. This tree in bloom was magnificent. The flowers were large, the size of regular tulips, and were a yellowy, chartreuse color which blended into orange. It was a tall tree and covered with flowers. It was such a beautiful sight! I only remember seeing one other tree like it, in Connecticut. I enjoyed these canoe rides so much, but, of course, I was too young to paddle! Sometimes, on Sundays, as we didn't have any other forms of entertainment, both my parents and I paddled northward on the river, in the opposite direction from Brookview, and glided to a sand bluff, where, at some time in the past, the sand around the pine tree roots had been washed away, probably during a severe storm, leaving strange, contorted trunks and roots exposed. It was a wonderland, beautiful, as well as so great to play on.

Paddling the canoe to Brookview was for more than just procuring staples that we could not produce ourselves on the farm. We now had two cows, Possie, short for Oppossum and Lissie. Possie was a very gentle, lovable cow, but not her daughter, Lissie. She was a bad tempered brat and would love to kick over the milk bucket any time she found an opportunity. Once I came to stand in the doorway to admire Lissie's latest calf and before I knew it, I was no longer standing. I was on the ground, looking up at a very angry mother cow! My mother did all the milking of both cows which had to be done twice a day, mornings and evenings. My father tried it once, said the cows would not cooperate, would not give him any milk, and that was the end of his milking career! If we had stayed on the farm until I was older, probably a teenager, I would have also been recruited for the milking chores. I wonder how I would have made out. With Lissie, not too well, I expect! Anyway, Mama saved the cream we got from the milk from these cows and churned butter from it in a hand-operated churn. I would occasionally be requested to try my hand at this job, but I must admit I was not very good at it. Once the butter started to form, I could barely turn the churn handle at all and Mama had to finish the job. She had wooden moulds that contained exactly one pound of butter. These moulds were shaped like an upside down bowl, open on both ends. The top was a circular carved piece of wood with a handle attached, used to press the butter out of the mould. Ours had a nice three-dimensional pattern of oak leaves and acorns carved in intaglio on it. This would be transferred to the butter creating a distinctive design, so everyone would recognize it as Wentzel's butter. Mothers of my classmates instructed their kids to find out from me when Mama would be making butter. It was highly regarded and in great demand. As soon as Papa delivered it to the general store, it would be sold out!

At some time in the mid-thirties, my father purchased a car from one of his friends. It was a 1924 Durant, at that point about 10 or 12 years old. My father thought it would be nice to take me to the highway on rainy days to catch the school bus, so that I wouldn't have to go to school wet. That would have been about all that he could have done with it. He didn't have a drivers" license and the car had no plates, so taking it on the highway was completely out of the question. However, there was one hitch to this great plan—the car really only ran well on nice days! It didn't seem to want to go out in the rain either. Papa kept tinkering with it, not ready to admit defeat, yet. Once he told me to hold a screwdriver against a spark plug to see if it was as dead as he thought. It wasn't! I yelped and dropped the screw driver. He said "Hm, I was so sure that was the bad one. Guess not."

That 1924 Durant finally found its niche. Papa converted it into a very large chain saw and used it for the rest of our stay on the farm to saw up firewood. Only on nice days, of course!

CHAPTER 16

SEPARATE BUT HARDLY EQUAL

One day I saw Mr. Brown walking down the road to our house. I was going to run and greet him, but my mother told me to go in the house instead. I thought this was kind of strange. I knew Mr. Brown because he did odd jobs for some of our neighbors, and considered him my friend, even though he was black. He always talked to me and sometimes would leave a tiny boat or other object that he had carved where he knew I would find it. Mr. Brown also wove baskets to sell and did miscellaneous jobs for farmers in the area like, chopping firewood. He worked very hard to make a living. As the farmers on the Eastern Shore weren't really sure that the Civil War was actually over and that the Confederacy had lost, it was not at all easy for a black person to survive. Mr. Brown lived with his wife and baby daughter in an old school bus that had been abandoned in the woods. It seems strange now, but at the time, the Thirties, there was nothing unusual about abandoned vehicles. Apparently when they stopped running, they were left where they died. Farm equipment suffered the same fate. On our farm there were three or four really rusty cars scattered about, here and there. I liked to play in them and my father found them to be a great source of spare parts and pieces for his various projects and repairs. One project he had made for me was a one-child merry-go-round that he had made from an old wheel to which he had attached a swing. It was fun having a revolving swing, but as I had to swing myself and push at the same time to turn the wheel, it really not that simple. I would have enjoyed having a playmate or sibling who could have joined me on another swing on the opposite side of the wheel, but that never happened.

I have no idea how the bus came to die in the woods. On my birthday I found out why my mother sent me into the house. She had ordered a special basket from Mr. Brown which she didn't want me to see because I would have asked entirely too many questions. It had a handle that was off-centered. When mama sewed and installed a liner and attached a fabric hood to this handle and put ruffles all around the outside, it became a doll's bassinet. It was so pretty and I was certainly surprised! Mr. Brown sometimes chopped wood for us too, but even though the pay for chopping a cord of wood was very minimal, it would not be wise to pay him more than the going rate. My parents were not in a position to defy convention, having two strikes against them already; being German and being northerners from New York, to boot! Even the Beabouts were regarded with some suspicion. They, too, were foreigners. They came from CHICAGO! Mama, to ease her conscience, always fed Mr. Brown a really good meal and gave him plenty of food to take home to his family.

Although Maryland was a border state and had never joined the Confederacy, it was profoundly Southern even well into the Thirties. My girl friend Ann's great-grandfather was a Confederate veteran. Unfortunately, he was in his nineties when I met him and I couldn't understand a word he said, so I can't pass on any great stories from him. Black children were not permitted to attend school with whites. This was, of course, long before 1964 and Brown vs. Board of Education. As a consequence, most black children received no education at all, as there were so few schools for them and no buses at all to transport them there. My parents commented often on this sad state of affairs, but to no avail. Those kids remained completely illiterate if they stayed in Maryland. This was the South of the thirties!

One night a group of perhaps twenty negroes appeared at our door, begging to spend the night in our barn, as they had been chased out of the place they had been staying by a group of rowdy teenagers. Whether they were renters or squatters, we never found out, but in any case, this motley group of men, women and children had nowhere to go. Regretfully, my father had to send them away because he noticed that several of the group were smoking cigarettes. He feared that they might renege on their promise not to smoke. It was much too dangerous to have anyone smoke in a barn filled with a year's supply of hay, as well as two cows and a horse, none of which would survive a fire. It was far too great a risk to take. However, as winter had not yet set in, they would probably be O.K. spending the night in the woods. Mama gave them enough food for entire group, and wished them well as they left.

CHAPTER 17

SCAREDY CAT

My father was a rational man and had a low tolerance for superstitions, fears and other such nonsense. He was frequently at odds with my sister, who was his step-daughter. I have often heard him say to my mother, "How can she possibly believe such rubbish? It is hard to believe that anyone in the twentieth century is still in the dark ages like that." My mother would try to smooth things over between them by saying, "Now, Ernst, if that's the way she feels, we should respect her opinion, even though it is obviously not yours!" He would just shake his head and let it go. She wasn't his daughter. This put me in a somewhat precarious position. I was his daughter! I felt that what Lori believed in was probably not true, but who knew for sure? So many people had these little quirks. Broken mirrors would cause seven years of bad luck, don't walk under a ladder, etc. The ladder thing, I felt, might have some merit. There could possibly be a bucket of paint that a careless painter forgot to remove, somewhere above you! Of course, as a sensible and somewhat cautious kid, I was very careful never to mention this to my father, as I had a reputation to maintain. My father considered me an intelligent child. My mother would probably not have been so upset and taken it in stride.

One thing I never mentioned to either of them was that while I was not exactly afraid of the dark, but instead, somewhat apprehensive of darkness. I just wasn't comfortable outdoors in the dark. Indoors, I had no problems. The limited circle of light emitted by the kerosene lamps felt cozy and safe to me. Of course, when I say it was dark at night, it really was! If there was a full moon, there was moonlight, but that was it. The woods separated us from the highway, which was really only very dimly lit. We seldom went out at night, as our only transportation was the canoe, Papa's bicycle, and the horse drawn wagon. The last two options were out of the question to get all three of us out at night. The horse would have shied from the passing cars and their headlights, even though there would not have been many, but it would only have taken one. Julie, the horse, was not used to that sort of thing at all. And the bicycle was not built for three! That left the canoe, which we sometimes, not very often, paddled down to a friend's house, which was also located right on the river, just like ours.

On the trip home, we had to pass an abandoned farm. The house that was on this property looked spooky enough in daylight, as there was no longer any glass in the windows, but moonlight really made it look ominous! It sat on a bluff overlooking the river as we glided past. The house itself was bad enough, with its dead-looking windows starring at me, but as the practice in that part of the country was, family members were often buried right on their farm. The sight of those slightly askew tombstones gleaming white in the moonlight would have made any pre-adolescent kid very nervous! I didn't believe in ghosts, of course, but still I just did not like it. During daylight hours, the school bus passed some of these family graveyards, but that was O.K. They were usually surrounded by a nice fence, with polished brass rails which were inserted into granite corner posts. They looked very secure, there could be no escapees!

Getting back to the abandoned farm, even though it was much closer to our place than many of the other places I walked to with my dog, I never went there. I told myself my parents would not like me to. But that wasn't the real reason. There was only a small brook that separated that property from ours, which I could have easily walked across, but I never did. I know nothing about this farm, who had owned it or why they left. In the six years we lived on that farm, I never saw a human being anywhere near that place!

CHAPTER 18

SHOPPING

L iving on the farm, with no method of long distance transportation, my parents and I did not get around to the big cities and their stores very often. We were completely dependent on friends and neighbors who occasionally invited Mama and me to accompany them on their shopping expeditions to Cambridge or Salisbury, the county seats of Dorchester and Wicomico Counties respectively. This was a really big deal. It didn't happen often, maybe once or twice a year. Trips to the Big Cities, the ones with the stores! Woolworth's, in particular where I was permitted to wander around and examine each item, and finally allowed to pick one item that I really, really wanted. This was wonderful! In the department stores or other similar establishments, I was only permitted to look, not to touch. This was especially frustrating when we walked past toy stores. Mama said that I couldn't even go in just to look. If we did, she said, the clerks would insist on selling us something which we could not afford, so no, I could not go in. This was very, very hard. There was so much stuff on display in the windows which I would have loved to pick up and inspect more closely.

Once our neighbor, Mr. Palisado, invited Mama and me to accompany him to Salisbury. This sounded great to me. Although I never felt deprived, living in isolation on the farm without playmates, a trip to the Big City was always welcome. In this instance, however, it did not work out quite so well. We got as far as Mardela Springs, crammed into Mr. Palisado's truck, when the darned truck broke down. Luckily it was near a filling [gas] station, so he didn't have to push it very far. He and the gas station attendant worked on that truck all afternoon, and finally, just as the sun was setting, they got it running again. Just in time to turn around and head for home. Very disappointing, no visit to Woolworth's 5 and 10 or any place else!

I will always have a soft spot in my heart for Woolworths'. I still miss it! When I was very little and we were still living in City Island, my mother would sometimes take the bus to Fordham Road or West Farms to go shopping, dragging me along. Fordham Road was by far my favorite. There was a Woolworths' there! Not so at West Farms. As far as I was concerned, it was a waste of time to take the bus all the way there. Once Mama bought me a tiny rattan furniture set for my dollhouse. There were four pieces, a sofa, two chairs and a table, all for a nickel. I was delighted and my mother was happy about the bargain. Not so my father, who said, "You should not patronize those stores. They can afford to sell stuff so cheap because the workers who made it probably get paid a bowl of rice for a day's work. That's certainly exploitation!" "Maybe so," Mama said, "But they are at least getting that bowl of rice, instead of starving, which might have happened if I hadn't bought there."

CHAPTER 19

ASTORIA

When I was eleven years old, my parents and my sister decided it would be nice for me to visit with Lori and her family in Queens, N.Y.C. for the summer vacation. My sister thought it would be a good idea for us to have a closer relationship, as normally I would only get to see her about once a year, when she, her husband and their little daughter Elinore would come to visit us on the farm and stay for a week or two. The rest of the year, I would fantasize how much fun we could have if she lived close by. I would pretend that we would take a ride in one of the derelict cars that were scattered around the farm, left at the spot where they died and never towed away. However, Lori was never consulted as to how she would feel, pretending to drive a rusty, immovable wreck. I seriously doubt if she would have been as delighted as I was, as she was at that point twenty-seven years old!

My parents probably thought I should get around more and experience more of city life instead of living such an isolated, introverted life and not having playmates during the summer months when school was not in session. They felt I really need more stimulation than the animals and plants that were available could provide. Of course, we had lots of books, which I read and reread. They were not childrens' books, although I had those, too, but no longer read them, preferring instead to read the miscellaneous assortment of literature that my parents had collected during the years before the depression. I remember reading "Beau Geste" every summer for three or four years. I also read "Lorna Doone" when I was eight, an amazing coincidence. It was the first novel I ever read and also the first modern novel ever written! I didn't understand that much of it, but that was never a deterrent for me. The physical act of reading was what attracted me and I read it all the way through! My mother thought perhaps I should be a little more up-to-date and ordered a subscription to the "Saturday Evening Post" for me. This wasn't exactly a kid's magazine, either, but I enjoyed it and my parents did, too, and we had interesting discussions about various stories. Most of these stories were divided up into two or three installments, so there was always something to look forward to with anticipation. Each story ended with "To be continued."

Well, Lori and her family came down to visit us on the farm for a week and then it was time for us to head back north to Astoria, New York City. Mama packed the clothes she thought I should take with me in an old suitcase that had originally come with us from Germany and was, by now, pretty beat up. I had no idea what to pack, as I had never gone anywhere before, so my mother made the decisions for me. In those days, kids did not decide what to wear. Mothers decided! I did not much care, as long as it was comfortable, I would wear it. She included several dresses she had sewed herself. Actually they were cut from the same paper pattern, using different materials, so, to the untrained eye, they all looked different. Both the pattern and the fabrics had been ordered from Sears Roebuck and had come by mail. This was fine with me, as I had practically no fashion sense at all. I wore the shoes I had on, as new shoes had always been a problem for me. Previously, Mama drew an outline of my feet on a sheet of paper and enclosed it with the order to Sears. When the new shoes arrived and I tried them on, I almost always complained that they didn't fit and had to be returned. Mama was not happy about this and tried to persuade me that they really didn't really hurt, but I was adamant, they had to go back and exchanged for the next larger size. This was probably the reason that my shoes for New York came from an actual shoe store. My feet had grown to a size six. Six was considered a lady's shoe size. Girl's shoes stopped at size five, so these shoes came with heels! My mother was shocked, an eleven-year-old in high heels! Not that they were really high, only about an inch. Mama said, "Can you really walk in those?" I proudly said, "Sure". I knew full well that, in September, when school started again, these very same white shoes would have to be dyed black by my mother, because you just couldn't wear white shoes after Labor Day. They would smell really bad for a few weeks, and everyone in the school would know that you didn't have new shoes for the beginning of the school year. Later in the year, when it got colder, Mama had to stuff the shoes with old newspapers because the soles were starting to disintegrate, and Papa could no longer fix them with the shoe repair tools he had ordered from Sears. But that was O.K. nobody could smell that!

So, now we were ready to leave. We piled into my brother-in-law, Adolf's car, the four of us and a kitten that my sister had taken a fancy to. This was long before seat belts and the kitten wandered all over the car and its occupants. It seemed like an endless trip to me and to my four-year old niece, even though it is only about 200 miles. As we came to our destination, I was amazed that the houses were so close together. I had forgotten what cities actually looked like. As we got into Astoria, the homes had front porches that were mostly windows with lots of little panes. There were streets after streets with dozens of these little houses with their tiny-paned windows. I wondered if my sister lived in one of them. Those cookie-cutter homes looked like only one architect had designed all of Astoria. But she didn't. We stopped in front of a three-story apartment house. They lived on the top floor. We all trooped in, including the kitten. I was amazed and thrilled with this apartment, everything in it looked new! Back home, nothing looked new. Nothing was!

My mother had given me a five dollar bill for spending money when I left for New York. That impressed me very much because in my lifetime, I had seen very few five dollar bills, especially if they were mine! I put it in a little wooden bank, shaped like a barrel. And there it stayed because my sister would not let me spend it. If I wanted to buy a toy or candy, she said I shouldn't waste it on something so frivolous. Even when my socks became more and more holey and I wanted to buy a new pair, she said, "Don't do that. What will Mama say if I let you use your own money to buy socks. You can darn those socks, they aren't that bad." In those days, little girls were expected to do needlework, which included darning socks. I was quite good at that. One stitched around the hole and then wove the yarn back and forth until the hole was completely filled in. Just because I was good at it doesn't mean that I really liked to do it, but my sister insisted. I know that she really didn't have the money, even though her husband now had a steady job. He was a chef who had apprenticed at one of the finest hotels in Frankfurt. He, too, had been hit hard by the Depression. He was happy to have this job, but it was hardly gourmet cooking. Adolf was the chef at Hector's Cafeteria on Times Square, but it was a steady job. At the beginning of the depression, there was no way he could count on having work every day. The employment agencies had the job market pretty well sewed up, and they would send him to a job opening. After he had worked for two weeks without any complaints about his work, the employer would fire him, without any reason. But he still owed the agency a week's pay. After he returned to this agency, or any other, He would be sent out on another job, frequently the same one he had just been fired from. They were happy to rehire him, and the whole process was repeated. Who knows how many other workers were caught up in this vicious cycle! But even though things had improved a lot and they could now afford this nice apartment as well as a car, they still had to be very careful not to overspend. As I was only a child during the depression, I did not experience the heartache of unemployment first hand, but I did listen and many of the stories which were told and retold.

In all the time we lived on the farm, January 1931 to August 1937, I only went to the movies there once. The whole school was taken by bus to see "Peck's Bad Boy" in a neighboring town. It was very nice to be taken some place instead of being stuck in a classroom, but I have no idea why. Anyway, everyone had a good time and enjoyed the film. In Astoria, I was taken to the movies a number of times, mainly because movie theaters were AIR CONDITIONED! This was a real novelty, because almost nothing else was. Certainly not homes or cars or subways. I don't believe stores had air conditioning, either. Theaters advertised on their marquees, "Air Conditioned—20 degrees cooler inside." This was a powerful draw. The movie playing at the time was in much smaller print below. No one cared all that much about the picture, the audience flocked there to enjoy the cold air, because summer in N.Y.C. can be brutal.

The movie I remember best, not because of the plot or even who starred in it, but because it was in Techicolor! I had not even known that movies came in color. I was delighted. The plot, what little I recall of it was set in Mexico with beautiful senoritas in bright exquisite costumes, and of course, the dashing caballeros. I was absolutely enthralled ! I would have watched that explosion of color over and over, but my family thought otherwise and we all went home to my sister's apartment. I believed that this apartment was just so perfect, at least when compared to the decrepit farmhouse we lived in at home. Not a crack in the walls, the windows, when opened, stayed that way, the paint looked new and beautiful, and the furniture was lovely. My sister was a very fussy person and had excellent taste, so everything had to be just right.

CHAPTER 20

MORE OF THE SUMMER IN ASTORIA

The summer in Astoria went on and on. The Triboro Bridge had been completed early in the summer and had been officially opened with a proper ribbon-cutting ceremony by President Franklin D. Roosevelt. Beneath the access to the bridge lay Astoria Park, newly developed to coincide with the opening of the bridge in 1936. The park was quite large, extending all the way to Ditmars Blvd, where my sister and her family lived. This park included Astoria Pool, which was a daily destination for four-year-old Elinore and me. Kids were admitted free every weekday morning and you can be sure that we were there promptly at 9 A.M. every morning that Lori had not made other plans for us, such as shopping. The pool was lots of fun, I didn't mind the baby sitting chore at all. At the time baby sitting did not even officially exist. Older kids watched the younger kids, that was a given. Ellie was no problem for me, only once did we have a difference of opinion. She, being only four years old, was naturally a bit shorter than I was at eleven, but still she felt that it would be fine for her to jump into the pool at the deep end, which was about four feet deep. She would not listen to me that the water was above her head and jumped in anyway! I realized at once that I should stop laughing because she looked so funny standing there, completely submerged, and jump in myself to pull her out. She was not very happy, but I was able to say, "I told you so!" When you are eleven, all little kids are so dumb! She got even, though. By the time she was twelve, she was already taller than I!

Elinore and I were not very excited about going shopping as neither of us had any great interest in clothes. However, Department Stores were nice. They had escalators which were great fun to ride up and down. I guess I had never ridden on one before, because I dragged Ellie around for the rides endlessly. Once, I lost track of which floor my sister was shopping on, but felt that this information should not be shared with my little niece, so we kept riding up and down, while I was scanning floor after floor, trying to find my sister! I finally did, and breathed a sigh of relief. Ellie never noticed how nervous I was getting and did not cry.

We also shopped locally on Steinway street, the shopping mecca of Astoria. It was a long walk to get there from Lori's home, but very interesting. There were stores on both sides of the street which had lovely merchandise on display, including toys. We liked those. On one occasion when my sister had some money [she had bought me socks in the meantime] we stopped at an embroidery shop and she bought me a tiny pillow case and a small comforter which I was to embroider. It was printed with two bunnies dancing around on each of them, which were to be embroidered in various colored yarns. The original print disappeared in the first wash. I already knew how to embroider and was very pleased to receive these gifts. So, now just sitting on the stoop in front of the apartment house, I could sit there and embroider these linens for my doll's bed. The pillow case came out very nice, but, as the comforter was larger, the stitches I used also automatically became bigger and somewhat less attractive.

The last time I was in Dallas visiting little Elinore, who, strangely enough, by this time had somehow become an elderly lady, she showed me the comforter and asked me if I knew who had made it. I laughed and said, "Don't you remember? I sat on your stoop in 1936 and embroidered it! There was a pillow that went with it. What happened to that?"

The summer of 1936 was very, very hot. Somehow, I had gotten a stomach virus, which did not add to my comfort factor at all, as the only way to cool off was to go to the pool or the air-conditioned movies, and neither of those options were open to a kid with an upset stomach. My brother-in-law said it was my own fault, I had drunk a glass of ice water. Apparently, folk-lore at the time was that you could get sick from drinking something cold, or maybe it was just his German prejudice against American customs coming to light. Even today, visitors from Germany are horrified at the idea of putting ice in their drinks! I wonder how come ice cream is exempt. Luckily the virus didn't last long, and it was back to the pool on week days and the movies on weekends.

But summers do come to an end and I was ready to go back to Maryland and Eldorado School. However, no one was available to take me. I had spent the last three weeks of summer with family friends, Aunt Grete and Uncle Rudy, in City Island. They had a little boy, Ralphie, who was about two or three years old. He was a pretty nice kid, except when he got angry, then he would bite. I quickly learned to avoid him when he got mad! The atmosphere was nicer in City Island, more small town in feeling. The houses were mostly single family with nice yards and flowers everywhere and we were right by the ocean. I liked being so close to accessible water. It was so different from the pool.

Now it was really time for me to go home, back to my parents and the farm, not to mention school. Somehow the grown-ups had forgotten to plan for that! Uncle Rudy and Aunt Grete had some friends in Tarrytown, N.Y. who were traveling south, and it was decided they would take me home. I was very shy at age eleven, and, as these people were strangers to me, I didn't speak to them unless they asked me a question. They must have found this odd, and said to each other, "Doesn't that kid ever talk?"

CHAPTER 21

MY ANIMAL FRIENDS

When I finally returned from my visit to New York, I was warmly greeted by both of my parents, as well as my animal friends on the farm. My dog, Dina, was ecstatic, jumping about and running in circles around me. The cats took my arrival in stride, pleased, but not overwhelmed. The family of Bantam chickens also seemed happy. They saw my return as an opportunity to come beg for more food. In the past March I had been given a Bantam rooster and two hens by a neighbor. These are pretty, little red chickens with black iridescent tails. They are only about half the size of regular chickens. Both hens had made nests and laid tiny eggs in them. These had hatched, and now I had a flock consisting of seven small chickens. They knew who I was and what time I was due to arrive home from school. They would be waiting for me to feed them by hand! The cows and the horse were non-committal.

I have always had good rapport with animals, in fact, sometimes a lot better than with humans. Animals are never deceitful and never leave you in doubt where you stand with them. If they dislike you, it will not be kept a secret, you will definitely know! When we were back in the city and I would go for walks with my mother and happened to see a cat, she would always caution me, "Don't speak to it, or it will follow us home, and I don't want to take in someone else's cat!" When necessary, I could persuade most cats who were stuck in a tree, out on a limb, to come back down. Dogs are fine, too. When we lived in Key Largo, we were on the second floor, as most houses down there are two stories, with the living quarters above the garage to keep out the water in the event of hurricane flooding. That never happened in the twenty years that we lived there. Anyway, my husband and I would frequently have our meals on the screened front porch and would greet friends if they happened to walk by. If they were walking a dog, which they usually were, many of the dogs refused to budge unless my husband or I, or preferably both of us, came down the spiral staircase to greet the dog personally!

We were also on very good terms with the neighborhood cats. One in particular, Max, who lived across the street, would always flick his tail in greeting, when we called out to him, "Hello, Max!" His housemate, Barney, was so eager to come in and visit that he chewed holes in three of our four screen doors. The fourth one was saved only because it was in back of the house and Barney was unaware of its existence. This was a bit scary until we found out who the culprit really was. Our first thought had been squirrels or possibly even rats! We were very happy to find out that it was just a very determined cat who was caught in the act! Jill, who owned these two cats, as well as a Manx house cat, Fred, also had a brown Lab, one of the dogs who had to be personally greeted by us. For his birthday we gave Hershey, this dog, a large bone wrapped in comic strip paper. He knew exactly what was in it, and immediately began unwrapping it. It was so cute to watch him!

One of my more surprising animal encounters occurred in Manhattan during the 40s. I came across a police horse, standing by himself at the curb, unoccupied, so to speak, so I stopped to pet his nose. I then proceeded to go on my way into the side door to Gimbels Department Store, when I noticed that the horse was following me. Not wanting to be caught "Red-handed" as a horse thief, especially a N Y P D horse thief, I had to persuade him to return to his original parking spot. He was most reluctant!

My husband and I have also had some enlightening encounters with dolphins. Once we stayed at a motel on Sugar Loaf Key called the Sugar Loaf Motel, which had two dolphins in their pool, called, not surprisingly, Sugar and Loafer. The motel's dolphin trainer had quit his job and the dolphins were being fed by a grouchy old man, who had no interest in them what so ever. He had been hired to feed them and that was all he was going to do. He refused to interact with them, even though they tried to engage him in some sort of play. But to him this was just a job and he had no intention of doing any thing else. But their lives were really not so bad. They were able to create their own fun, regardless of the crabby guy. Whenever they noticed motel guests gathered around the pool, they immediately went into their routine, tossing a ball to each other, or playing with whatever they could find in the pool. Once an actor, always an actor, once again proving that there's no business like show business!

CHAPTER 22

HEALTH CARE

Why does everyone seem to be so sick? This is all I hear. Most of my friends and contemporaries, collectively, have almost every ailment known. Getting old is hardly a new phenomenon, people have been doing it for years and years. We never used to hear about all these bodily malfunctions. I am confused. Is it just that I have been so fortunate to be enjoying better health than most folks?

Children's health insurance would have been totally wasted on me. When I was four years old and we were still living the good life in City Island, high on the hog, so to speak, my mother took me to a doctor, who said my tonsils should be taken out. I did not like the sound of this one bit. I did not think that having body parts removed was for me! Turned out that it sure wasn't. The year was 1929, Papa lost the good job he had for two years and was unable to find another of any sort. So, of course, there had been no money for unnecessary operations. Even today my tonsils remain firmly attached to my throat. Oh, I've had a few sore throats and colds through the years, but nothing very serious, and none lately, not in the past five years.

When I was in Kindergarten, still on City Island, all the children in the whole school were vaccinated against diphtheria. There had probably been an outbreak of this dreaded disease at the time. Anyway, the nurses came and gave shots to all the kids, class by class. This was done in the schoolyard for some reason. We, the Kindergarten class, were extremely proud. Nobody cried! It was a great triumph for us because the first graders all cried, even some of the second and third graders cried, but not us! Even the teachers were impressed. There was a great feeling of mass solidarity among us. It felt great to be a part of such a brave group!

When we relocated to Maryland, that was the end of any outside medical attention. My mother had been a nurse during the First World War in Germany and consequently was able to take care of whatever minor problems came up. I thoroughly disliked her cure for sore throats, which consisted of wrapping a cold, wet, wool sock around the neck and pinning it in place. I hated it and always tried to hide that my throat hurt from my mother. But she was good, always found out and got out the sock!

When I was about nine or ten, a measles epidemic swept through the school. It started a few weeks before Christmas, just as the principal lined up the cast for the annual P T A Christmas play. I wasn't in it, of course, as we had no way to get to the school at night. I didn't mind that very much, but I really did resent the busy work that non-cast members were assigned to do during rehearsals. I reverted to my usual approach and spent most of my time listening and mentally rewriting the lines, and not doing the assignment.

It seemed that every time the cast learned their lines reasonably well, an important actor came down with the measles and had to be replaced. This went on for several weeks, much to the principal's frustration. The choice of healthy actors was becoming slimmer and slimmer. I suppose the play did go on, somehow, as it was finally Christmas. Ah, Christmas holidays, no school! My sister had sent a package from New York and it looked like a wonderful week was coming up. I opened my packages on Christmas Eve and was delighted with my gifts. Papa lit the candles on the tree and we sang Christmas carols and ate candy. What could possibly be nicer? On Christmas morning, I woke up to find that I had no interest in playing with all the lovely stuff I had received, actually only wanted to go back to sleep. I couldn't understand it, but my mother did. Measles!

Mama fixed me a bed in the living room, so that I could see the Christmas tree, but I really didn't care. The room was kept fairly dark, so as not to ruin my eyes, therefore I slept most of the time. Once I woke up suddenly from a dream of playing with one of my dolls and I groggily said, "Where is my doll? I can't find her, she was just here." Mama probably didn't realize that I had been sleeping and insisted that I was delirious.

She told Papa that he would have to set out at first light and get a doctor. There was a doctor in Galestown, but that was many miles away and it had been snowing steadily for a few days. I kept insisting that I had been dreaming and wasn't delirious at all, but Mama wouldn't listen. She thought I was too delirious to know that I was delirious! Papa set out on foot first thing in the morning, but the snow was too deep and he didn't get very far into the woods before he had to return. Actually there was no way of knowing if the highway had been cleared or even if the doctor had been available, would he have been able to get through the snow on the dirt roads.

So I continued to sleep and eventually got better on my own, played with my new toys, and went back to school when it reopened in the new year.

CHAPTER 23

RECYCLING THE TRASH

My father once recycled a bridge. Sometime in the early 30s, a new steel bridge was built across the Marshyhope Creek between Eldorado and Brookview. When it was completed, the workmen just cut apart the old wooden bridge and let the pieces float downstream. These were really nice 10 x 10 timbers and my father just couldn't see letting them go to waste. They would surely be a navigational hazard as well. In any case, he launched his canoe, the only boat we had and paddled downstream in hot pursuit to lasso those precious pieces of wood. He managed to maneuver most of them to the shore, where he beached each one on a low spot and then went after the next one. He was able to collect quite a lot of them. I really don't know how many, I was only seven at the time, but it seemed like there was big pile.

Now, what to do with them? About a hundred feet away, where the riverbank was higher, he dug a pit, approximately 10 ft. by 10 ft. and about 8 ft. deep. This was to become the cellar of the smokehouse Papa was about to build with this salvaged lumber. He cut them to size where they were beached and then hitched Julie, the horse to each piece and dragged it to the pit. How he laid these heavy pieces of wood, one on top of the previous piece, I'm not sure, but he must have built an "A" frame and lifted each one with block and tackle. In retrospect, it seems like a tremendous job for one middle-aged man and one elderly horse!

The first roof was a sort of thatch made of corn stalks, but apparently that was not quite satisfactory. Later, a metal roof was ordered from

Sears Roebuck, and that worked out much better. Not much actual smoking of meat was ever done, even though Papa had installed a small smoker stove. I believe that there just wasn't enough smoke to preserve the meat well enough to last through the warmer weather, so my parents replaced the real smoke with fake smoke that came in a can and was rubbed into the meat. This was a much better preservative and lasted far longer. Steps led down to the lower section and that became a root cellar, where carrots, white potatoes, and sweet potatoes, as well as beets were stored for the winter. These had to be eaten while it was still cold outside, as in warmer weather the veggies would start to grow again! Of course, we also had the veggies my mother had preserved in Mason Jars, some of which were also stored on shelves in the cellar. These would actually keep for over a year if necessary, so there would be no rush to eat those.

We never had the amenities that city folks take for granted, certainly today, but even eighty years ago, such as telephones, electricity or running water. Well, yes, we did actually have running water, but it had to be pumped before it would run. It did not run from a faucet. There was also no garbage collection. Instead, the property came with a large pit that had been dug sometime in the distant past by a previous owner, into which was thrown anything that could not be reused for any purpose whatsoever. There were very few items in that category!

To begin with, there were no plastic bottles or bags, or anything made of plastic at all. Probably not many paper items, either. I don't remember if there were paper bags, but if there were, they were probably reused until they fell apart. Then they could be used as a fire-starter in the kitchen stove, along with other paper goods which would have been collected and carefully saved for this purpose. Sugar and flour came in cloth sacks, which when empty, were washed and bleached by my mother, to be ripped apart and used as towels and dish cloths. We never used chlorine. Instead, items to be bleached were laid, when wet, on the grass, to be bleached by the sun, completely free! There were no tin cans to be disposed of either, as we never bought any. If my father could grow it, my mother would can it, in the afore mentioned Mason Jars. If this wasn't possible, we just did without. Any organic by-products which would not be good for the pigs, were composted with the manure from the horse and cows. This left very little to be thrown into the pit, which really wasn't an eyesore at all, as it had acacia bushes growing all around it. They had lovely white flowers in the Spring, which also smelled heavenly. All that remained to be disposed of was broken glass, which we had very little of. One day I found an old light bulb that had floated down the river. I showed it to my mother, and she said, "Throw it into the pit, we have no use for that, but it might make a loud noise when it breaks!" I was contemplating a minor explosion, but no such luck, just the sound of breaking glass.

My sister had sent me a gift once, of six little dolls, three girls and three boys, about four inches tall. I had just recently learned to sew, and I made many little outfits for this crew to supplement the red plaid skirts and shorts that they were wearing when they arrived. One day I saw some fabric that looked very attractive to me laying on the sewing machine and I promptly cut out several little dresses from it. Later, Mama, very upset, said, "What have you done? I had cut out nightgowns for myself that I was going to sew later. Now you have ruined that for me! Why didn't you at least ask?" She was very angry indeed, which was unusual for her as normally she was a very calm person. Well, I always had this thing for scissors. I had always cut things out, as long as I can remember. Mama had always complained about the little snips of paper that always found their way to the floor. It just happened, it was fate!

I loved the old Sears Roebuck catalog. There were always pictures of children that could be cut out and used as paper dolls. They all had different clothes. Some of them, regrettably, had arms missing when a group was posed with arms behind someone else. I could always cut out the whole group to avoid this. My mother liked to hide her scissors from me by keeping them on a high dresser, when I was still too short to see the top. However, she made the mistake of placing a nice, shiny, chrome-plated kerosene lamp on this same dresser which reflected everything on its top surface. Little fingers had no trouble reaching the scissors!

CHAPTER 24

THE RIFLE

When my father had been in the German Army during the First World War, he was a sharpshooter, and even after he had been discharged, he still won many prizes as a marksman. Of all of these, my mother valued the sterling silver spoon the most, as that was actually useful. My mother had absolutely no use for guns at all, in contrast to my father, who really thought they were quite cool, as many guys do. When Papa left for America, he left his revolver in my mother's care, and said, "Keep it handy, as it might happened to be very useful, as you will have to sell off the remaining gold wedding and engagement rings, before you leave for New York with the girls. Who knows what kind of riff-raff might come to the door. You could use it to scare them off!" He knew that she would never actually use it, but thought it could be used as a deterrent. My mother said nothing at the time, but as soon as he left, she tossed the gun into the lake, and smiled as she watched it sink to the bottom.

A year later my mother, my sister and I emigrated to New York, without the gun, of course. I suppose most of the rings were sold. Years went by. The great Depression came and we moved to the farm in Maryland. There Papa felt that he might have use for a shotgun. I don't recall that he used it much. He tried to scare off the crows with it, but the crows were much too clever. They were probably laughing. Papa would plant three or four kernels of corn and heap the soil into a little hill around them. The crows would watch and follow at a distance and then dig up the kernels and eat them. Papa would fire the shotgun in their direction, but never hit them. You can't hit a crow! They would fly off, cawing their complaints, and return to their digging a short time later. My father swore that they could always tell the difference between a gun and some other long-handled tool, and paid no attention to the sight of a hoe or a rake, and totally ignored anything that wasn't a gun.

One day some friends came by, bringing with them tin cans and a rifle. We all, except Mama, amused ourselves by shooting at the cans thrown in the river. My father was impressed with my aim and decided to order a rifle from the Sears catalog, so that Mama and I would have some protection when he left us alone on the farm for the summer, to see if he could find work in New York. Quite a responsibility for an eleven-year-old who had never killed anything larger than a mosquito! I did eliminate a large number of mosquitos, as they bit me everywhere, it was a never-ending battle, but on the plus side, they never seem to want to bite me now, preferring almost anyone else to me!

The summer dragged on and on. I spent a lot of time practicing aiming at paper targets, which had also come from Sears and I had nailed to a clothes pole adjacent to the river, so that if I missed the target altogether, the bullet would land harmlessly in the water. This did not happen very often, as I was actually a pretty good shot. But without any competition, this was not a very exciting way to spend the hot days of summer. If I had a really good target, I brought it to my mother to show her and she was suitably impressed, but no way would she even go anywhere near that rifle, let alone touch it. Once a snake crossed my path, and for no good reason, I fired at it. After I saw that I had missed, I was so relieved and happy, because I have no idea why I fired at it. As the snake slithered away, I asked myself why I had done that. I still don't know, but I'm still glad. The snake was no threat to me, it was all so pointless!

Jumping forward about five years, we were back in New York, when the attack on Pearl Harbor took place, and we were at war! Suddenly we became Enemy Aliens, because my parents had never become U.S. citizens in order to preserve the tiny pension my father received from the German government as a wounded veteran. Well, that was gone now, and all enemy aliens were require to turn in firearms, cameras and short wave radios. We didn't have a short wave radio, probably weren't in existence in 1928, when our radio was purchased, so we were O.K. on that, but I did own two cameras, a Kodak Brownie from the 20's and a small camera I had received by collecting points from the corner candy, bread and milk store. They had to go! Mama took them to the Police Station. That left the firearms, my rifle and Papa's shotgun. My mother had never been very comfortable having them in the house, and I think that she was secretly happy to get rid of those things, and it wouldn't even be her fault! It was a Federal Regulation. I have no idea how she got the guns to the police station. She must have carried them. We could not have afforded a taxi. It would have taken her at least twenty minutes. I would really have liked to see that!

CHAPTER 25

BACK TO THE CITY

My father arrived back home from New York towards the end of the summer of 1937. He was very pleased that he had found suitable work, and, mistakenly thought the depression was finally over. It wasn't, but of course he couldn't know that then. The job he had secured was just a blip, not the real end of the depression. It did give him the confidence to go back to the city to try get a good job at work he loved, making quality jewelry, and once again being able to support his family properly. So now it was time to pack up.

Most of our belongings had come a long way; first across the Atlantic to City Island and then down to the Eastern Shore of Maryland. Each new residence provided an opportunity to add more furniture. The guy that Papa had hired to take the furniture from City Island to Maryland took one look at the puddle-ridden dirt road that led from the highway to the farm, shook his head and said,"This is as far as I can go. I'm unloading the stuff right here!" That left my father to carry the furniture on his back the rest of the way by himself, as he had no other way to transport it. This is what I was told. I wasn't there to see it myself.

Getting back to New York was a bit easier. My father hired a trustworthy person with a reliable truck, who went the distance. My mother and I, along with Dina, the dog had already left on the train to New York. My parents had sold off whatever we were unable to take with us. The livestock, the cows, the horse and the chickens were sold. The cats were given to neighbors, with whom we really hoped they would stay and be happy, and not return to the empty farm house. The dog went with us. She couldn't believe that Mama would actually make her suffer the indignity of wearing a harness and walking on a leash. She had always had complete freedom. She did not like this turn of events at all and promptly sat down and would not budge! It took her quite a while to get used to this restraint. The property was entrusted to a realtor, who was supposed to sell it, which he did, but neglected to send most of the money to my parents.

One hilarious incident comes to mind. Word got around that among other items, Papa was selling the canoe. Two portly gentlemen appeared at our door one morning. It was a bit cool. so they were wearing heavy jackets, boots and socks, and carrying their shotguns as well. They had come to try out the canoe, to see if they wanted to buy it. Papa cautioned them to be very, very careful when they were getting on board. This was not a rowboat, it was so much easier to tip over! They, of course, paid no attention and jumped right in. That was a mistake, as fast as they got in, the canoe tipped over, dumping them and their shotguns right into the water! They were in no danger, the water was only about two or three feet deep, but they sure got wet. Needless to say, they did not buy the canoe!

My father's bicycle also was sold. I was really sorry to see that go, although I do not remember who bought it. Even though it was a man's bicycle, adult size, I learned to ride it when I was eight years old. I had always been fascinated by wheels. I would have loved nothing better than having a pair of roller skates. Once when I was still very young, I found some casters in with my father's junk and tried to make my own skates on a cardboard base. Needless to say, these were a complete failure! Even if I had somehow, miraculously acquired skates, it still would have been impossible to skate on sand ! Sand was everywhere. To get back to the bicycle, I asked Papa if I might ride it. He said, "Sure". Probably he wondered how I would be able to do that. I had a method. The front porch was perched on cinder blocks, as was the rest of the house, but as there was no screen to obstruct access, I could take this large bike to the edge of the porch, hop on, as I was now able to reach the pedals, and pedal it as far as I could go up the road before the tires were buried in sand and I would have to jump off. Then I pushed back to the porch and started the same process all over again. Eight-year-olds are easily amused, because I could do this, over and over!

Mama had found a railroad apartment for us, a cold-water flat with six rooms, without central heating for twenty five dollars a month. They were called railroad apartments because one room led to the next like railroad cars. No hallway. An architectural masterpiece! The building was so old that it still had functioning gas lines to every room, although electricity had been installed with the wires exposed at a later date. Conditions were not as great as Papa expected. Work as a jeweler was impossible to find and he had to take a job as a dishwasher which my brother-in-law had helped him find. Even a menial job which paid $13.50 a week was treasured. On the plus side, he ate in the cafeteria where he worked so that was a saving!

The apartment in Astoria was no worse than most of the others in the neighborhood. Nobody had money. Someone with an actual job, no matter how badly it paid, was considered fortunate. Certainly much better off than the guys who had to go on relief, or work for the WPA, the Work Progress Administration. The fellows on WPA were made the butts of many jokes, such as; each job required at least five men, one to man the shovel and the other four to watch! Despite this, their accomplishments were many. Lots of public buildings, such as post offices, libraries and schools were put up by them. There was also a division which created murals in public buildings and completed smaller works of art.

My father worked nights, which allowed him, when he came home in the mornings, enough time to practice working on jewelry, using base metals, as the price of gold and silver were not in our budget, although compared with today's prices, they sure were bargains. If I had been working on a painting the night before and Papa saw the unfinished painting, he promptly finished it, much to my annoyance! In his jewelry making, he used a soldering torch which he connected to one of the conveniently available gas lines. Frequently, with an open flame, the curtains Mama had so carefully selected and hung caught fire. Like all jewelers' hands, Papa's were practically fireproof from callouses, so he simply clapped his hands around the flames and put out the fire. The curtains, much to my mother's disgust, were beyond repair. Complaining did her no good, my father insisted that the windows should have been bare in the first place. "But Ernst, they face the street," she said "What will the neighbors think?"

To make some extra money, my parents took in roomers from time to time. These were mostly workers from the cafeteria who needed a place to stay. Some of them I remember, because they were unforgettable. There were the bed-wetting brothers, who did not stay long, and then there was Schneider, the butcher. Him, nobody could forget. One morning, he said to my Dad, "You know, Ernst, when I came home on the subway last night, people were looking at me very funny. I didn't like that. I think I should have let them have it, but there were so many of them. Do you think I should have gotten rid of them? I do have my butcher knives." "No, no", Papa said, "You did absolutely the right thing. Now go to bed and get some rest, you will feel much better when you wake up. But don't drink any more beer." Schneider, while a nice quiet man, did like his beer, but he never seemed drunk, so nobody was very concerned. About an hour later, Papa and I, Mama was not home, were startled to hear the sound of breaking glass. My father said to me, "Stay here, I'll go look." He couldn't believe what he saw. Schneider was systemically throwing the furniture out on to the street through the closed window. My father screamed at him to stop, but he only paused long enough to say, "Don't you see them? They are all out there, in the street and standing on the sidewalk over there. I've got to get them!" We didn't have a phone, but someone on the block must have, and called the police. They finally arrived and took Schneider away. My mother came home just as he was being put into the police van, and then she saw the broken furniture in the front yard and almost fainted. Her husband and child had been in this apartment with a maniac! After she saw that we were both OK, even though the yard and the front room were in shambles, she relaxed a bit and put on some coffee. That's when the doorbell rang. It was a Western Union delivery boy with a telegram from Adolf, my brother-in-law. It read, SCHNEIDER CRAZY STOP GOT DRUNK STOP FIRED TOOK HIS KNIVES STOP WATCH OUT STOP. We had already found this out!

CHAPTER 26

LIFE GOES ON

Things were relatively quiet for a few years. Schneider had been taken away to Pilgrim State Hospital for the Insane. We later heard that he had died a few days thereafter, possibly because he had been badly beaten by the police. Unnecessarily, because he had put up no resistance, Mama said, as she had witnessed the whole thing. The broken windows had been repaired by the landlord and the debris in the yard had been cleared out. The only remaining souvenir was an alarm clock that had landed on the porch roof and kept right on ticking for many years.

Then came Pearl Harbor and the Second World War. We suddenly became Enemy Aliens because my parents had never become U.S. Citizens, in order to keep the tiny pension my father received from the German government as a wounded war veteran of the First World War. We were therefore required to register with the authorities and received the little pink booklets, which we were supposed to carry with us at all times. The Board of Education of New York City also decreed that all students were to wear around their necks the I.D. tags that had been issued to them. "Around your necks," the teacher said. "Not your wrists! What if your hand was blown off. How could you be identified?" We asked, "What if our heads were blown off?"

I was terrified by war as I had been brought up on war horror stories from the World War I, when my father had been in the German Infantry and my mother had been an Army Nurse. She worked in a hospital. Women were not permitted to be in the service at that time. Her stories guaranteed that I would never, ever be a nurse. The terrible condition of the soldiers' wounds would forever be etched into my mind. This was not for me! No blood, guts or maggot infested wounds to be cleaned; this was not for me. I could never take that! The eternal talk about the lack of food was also not pleasant to hear as often as I did, but it was, at least not morbidly depressing. I actually did not become upset when my parents insisted that all they had to eat was turnips, boiled turnips, turnips fried, turnips roasted, turnip coffee, turnip cake. Maybe a bit boring, but I never was an enthusiastic eater, and I really LIKED turnips. In Florida, they are called rutabagas.

But life went on in Astoria and elsewhere. I was attending a girls' high school in Manhattan, Julia Richman. I did not know any boys who were in the service and I didn't hang out much with the neighbors. My social life centered around school life. After school there was homework and school projects, and of course, chores. Therefore, I spent most of my time by myself and my family. Before I entered high school, I had actively disliked school. Eldorado, in Maryland and, Junior High 126 in Queens were boring and regimented to me. High school had been represented to us by our teachers as a depressing place, where much more would be demanded of us, and we would soon come to appreciate how good our lives were in the lower grades. They could not have been more wrong! I was delighted with high school, we had so much more freedom. We did not have to march through the hallways in perfect formation, never looking either left nor right and certainly never uttering a word. Homework was optional, as long as the assigned work was committed to memory, it did not actually have to be written down! This was great, just what I had been searching for all my life, without even knowing it! Had I known this all along, I would certainly made more effort to go to college. As it was, I really had no interest in college. My parents did not encourage me in this direction, as my father had college graduates washing dishes right alongside him in the cafeteria. They concluded that a college education was of no great use in America, so why go to the expense. I found out later that I could have taken summer classes that would have given me enough credits to go to one of the free city colleges, but my grade advisors never mentioned this. My advisor at Julia Richman found me a low-paying boring job, and my advisor in Junior High thought I should be going to church! Not a whole lot of help there.

But, back to class in the early days of the war, one day our teacher asked for volunteers to help distribute ration cards for gasoline. I raised my hand, as did a lot of girls in my class. We all had our jobs, checking credentials and other papers of the car owners who came in for their ration coupons. We were only assigned to work on gas coupons, although meat, sugar, butter and shoes were also rationed. This is what I recall, but the rations were really quite generous, I believe my mother always had left-overs at the end of the month. Anyway, the teacher treated us to lunch which was so exciting, we rarely got to eat out and actually order from a menu. After lunch, back in the classroom which had been put to use as a coupon distribution center, the teacher found that some kind of error had been made and that it was necessary to call one of the clients back. She selected my friend, Esther and gave her the message and a nickel and the number to call. My friend was terrified, "Please come with me", she begged. In all of her seventeen years she had never had occasion to use a phone and had no idea how they worked! I didn't either, of course, but that didn't stop me. I went with her, inserted the nickel and dialed. When the man answered, I gave him the message, just as if I had always been doing that! My friend was so happy, a great weight had been lifted off her shoulders. Fast forward seventy years, can anyone imagine anything like that happening today?

CHAPTER 27

FRUGALITIS

I have a disease that I am willing to own up to having. It has many names, but I call it G D I F, Great Depression Induced Frugalitis. Its symptoms are easy to recognize, it is the chronic inability to throw anything away, no matter how useless it may appear. If you keep something long enough, the time will come when you can improvise a use for it. If, for any reason, you should succumb to common sense and actually toss it out, you will regret that decision, for within two weeks you will find a very good use for it, but by then it will be irrevocably gone. I said it was chronic, rarely curable, but, on the bright side, hardly ever fatal. The only fatalities that I know of were the unfortunate Collyer brothers. The able-bodied brother was killed when a six-foot stack of old magazines, which the brothers planned to read, soon, toppled over on him, leaving the disabled brother to starve on a pile of newspapers which had been kept so that the brothers could clip the interesting articles that they wished to save.

Everyone who suffers from this affliction has different fields of interest. My husband was addicted to saving miscellaneous metals. He had a pile of copper pipes which he bought when we lived in Tamarac, because some of the residents there had problems with their plumbing and had to have their PVC pipes replaced with copper. My husband, always alert to possible potential problems, immediately took measurements and purchased the copper pipes. Five years later, there still had been no leaks in the PVC pipes. When we sold the house and moved to Key Largo, the pipes accompanied us and found a new home in the garage. From time to time, Julius would come across them, stop to admire them, and say, "Someday they will be very useful." Twenty years later, when I was ready to sell that house, the pipes were still there. Copper prices were low at that time and they were hard to sell so instead I donated them to a wild animal shelter in Homestead. I'm sure they were put to good use and Julius would probably have approved.

My own weakness is paper. When I was a child on the farm, drawing paper was unavailable at the general store. The only paper they carried was composition paper with lines. Pictures drawn on that just simply did not look right, the lines would always interfere. It really pains me to throw out nice sheets of paper which still have a clean usable side. I have taken to putting them in with the recycled newspapers and magazines to ease my conscience. Small scraps of cloth are also very hard to dispose of, they could have so many uses! My mother often said, "For Heavens' sake, what could you possibly do with anything that small?" I replied, "Something might come up." Telephone wire scraps, that the telephone repair guy forgot to clean up, especially longer pieces have many, many applications which the manufacturer never thought of. They make great twist ties, don't fall apart, connectors, all kinds of things. Small pieces of wood are good, too. There is no end of what can be done with them.

When Julius and I got married, we bought an eight-milimeter movie camera. When camcorders became popular, I sold the movie camera, which had become a collectors' item by then, especially as it wasn't battery operated. It was spring wound and the spring always seemed to run down when there was any interesting action. I included all the accessories that I found but overlooked the holder that had come with it to hold the camera steady. I recently found that holder, and with the slight adaption of leather gaskets, cut from leather pieces left over from a vest I made about sixty years ago, it fits my little digital just fine.

CHAPTER 28

NAMES

Expectant parents almost always spend a lot of time and thought on what to name the new baby. Sometimes the baby arrives and Mom and Dad are still discussing the matter. Then it becomes a hasty decision because the authorities would really like to know what to write on the birth certificate. It doesn't matter to them what the final choice is, they just want to be able to list a name and finish the paperwork! Now the situation becomes critical, even though the parents had nine months, all the choices are still up in the air. Sometimes it becomes a matter of just grabbing a name and writing it down, even though the kid will be stuck for life with it! In my sister's case, there was an excuse. She had an unexpected set of twins. My sister had decided quite early on that she would have a girl, and her name was to be Rosemarie. However, she was presented with another little girl and that one had no name waiting for her. Should it be Annette or Annemarie or something else entirely? Decisions, decisions! She finally settled on Annemarie, much to the relief of the hospital records staff. Of course, as is usually the case, their names were immediately shortened to Rosie and Annie and that's what they are still known as, over 70 years later.

Elinore and I had come home from the pool, and Mama said to us, "Lori gave birth this morning, what did you two want?" We both immediately said, "A girl!" Mama answered, "How many?" We were shocked, there was more than one? No one had expected twins, not even Lori's doctor. *When* Adolf got the call that he was now the father of three girls, two of them unexpected twins, he was at work at the cafeteria, and was so surprised that he grabbed a hot pan out of the oven and badly burned his hand, as he forgot to grab a towel first! So exciting! I laughed to myself at the news. At thirteen years of age, I had been considered too young to know about pregnancies and all the other interesting facts of life. When I overheard Lori discussing her pregnancy with a friend, telling her to make sure that I did not hear of it inadvertently, I was extremely annoyed that she thought I wasn't old enough to know about such things. I said to myself, "I hope she has twins, boys. It would serve her right!" Turns out that I wasn't very good at putting spells on people, only half of my curse came true! Looking back to 1939, pregnant women tried everything to keep their pregnancies a secret. They wore large baggy clothes and usually only left the house at night in the company of their husbands. I had a couple of girlfriends in Junior High, who suddenly had babies in their homes. No mention was ever made that their mothers were expecting.

Getting back to nicknames, I actually gave myself one. My excuse is that I was really very young and just starting to talk. My mother named me Margaret, which was her name, but she was always known as Greta. My sister's name was actually Elinore Margaret, but she was called Lori. I have always felt that Mama should have named me Margaret Elinore and then I would have had a middle name, but she didn't. In Maryland, most people were known by their middle names, so I felt somewhat deprived by not having one. In the traditional German way, I was called Gretchen, the diminutive of Greta. This was apparently too big a mouthful for a toddler just learning to talk. It came out Deti. The whole family must have thought that was cute because the name stuck. My entire family, which at this point includes besides nieces; grand-nieces and nephews, innumerable spouses of same and their offspring and to all of them I am Aunt Deti. My husband didn't care for this, so to his family I am Aunt Margaret.

When we arrived in the United States and Mama enrolled me in Kindergarten, she told them my name was "Gretchen". They said, in their best New York accent, "Right, Gretchen". "No" said my mother, "Gretchen" with the proper German pronunciation. They said, "Yeah, Gretchen". Mama was horrified, so she said, "Never mind, call her by her name, "Margaret".

CHAPTER 29

HOW I ESCAPED

My parents had always been quite adamant about making sure that I remembered to speak and read German. On the farm in Maryland this had not been any kind of a problem, as there was seldom anyone else around to speak to me in English. School, of course was different, but I had learned to adopt whatever dialect folks around me were using in order not to be conspicuous and stand out from the crowd. I always blended in. My parents mostly spoke to me in German, but in time their German became more and more corrupted with English words which came to mind so easily. Therefore, which ever language the word in question was thought of first was the one used or some combination of both, "Germanish", perhaps?

In Maryland, in school, I became a Southerner, back in Astoria, I became a New Yorker. So speaking, obviously, was no problem, but reading books, another story! I much preferred English. It was so much easier and quicker. I avoided my father's old German books like the plague. And writing, forget writing altogether!

After we returned to Astoria, N.Y. in 1937, thinking, mistakenly, that the Depression was over, my mother heard that children could attend classes in writing German on Saturdays at the "Turn Halle", which was the venue for local German social affairs, etc. She promptly registered my niece, Ellie, and me. There was however a slight problem. I was twelve years old and the rest of the class, including Ellie, consisted of six year olds! I could hardly expected to be happy there. In addition, the teacher was teaching writing very old German script, which only my mother and her sisters still used. It probably had last been taught in the 1890s. I thought, what was wrong with Roman letters?

As I was pondering how to extricate myself and Elinore from this mess, as she did not like going there any more than I did. She was in the first grade and had her own problems. I was the one who walked her there, probably a couple of miles, so we were in this together. Suddenly opportunity knocked, loud and clear. An "Ah, Ha" moment appeared on the horizon! These lessons were just a front for the "Bund", a Nazi organization that had managed to infiltrate a very normal social club. I immediately told my mother we couldn't go there anymore. The teacher had tried to get me to join the older girls, the blue-eyed, blond pig-tailed crowd, and embroider stuff to sell. I had the blue eyes, but also short curly dark hair. The embroidery consisted of handkerchiefs with half swastikas embroidered in one corner. Who were they trying to kid? Half swastikas? Anyway, neither Ellie nor I ever had to go to those classes again!

CHAPTER 30

FAMILY HISTORY

The family history that I know I have gotten orally from my parents. Beyond their memories of what they know from their parents are shrouded in the mysteries of the past. So what I actually know goes back about 150 years. My father's father was born in Hamburg, his family must have been fairly well-to-do. I believe great-grandfather was a butcher. The reason I believe they were reasonably affluent is that I have a photograph of his entire family, parents and three sons, which I estimate was taken around 1862. I'm judging by my grandfather, who looks about seven years old. He died in 1925 at age 70, so doing the math leads me to 1862. In all probability poor people didn't take their families to be photographed by a professional, not that amateurs even existed. This was way before point-and-shoot. It involved a photographer under a black cloth, a very large camera, glass photographic plates, not film and a supply of flash powder, which was ignited to light up the scene. As everyone looks well-dressed in this photograph—Great-grandmother in voluminous hoop skirts, Great-grandpa in a nice suit, in a high-collared shirt and a floppy bow tie, the two older boys, Grandfather August and his older brother, Hermann, in matching uniform-looking suits, and baby brother Richard, still wearing a dress, as the style was for little boys until they went to school. Long curls, too, if they had any. Richard didn't!

My grandfather grew up to become a merchant, selling lots of miscellaneous items. One of his careers was as a ship's chandler. He would arrive at the ship to sell merchandise to the captain, properly dressed as a successful salesman to get the order. When the time came for delivery, he wore old clothes, a cap pulled down over his ears and pushing a wheelbarrow containing the goods. Thus he became the delivery man! He had a grocery store for quite a while, which Papa remembered best, as he could sit unnoticed behind a barrel and sneak candy from the counter! Papa's mother died when he was only three years old. She led a very hard life with many pregnancies, six, I believe. None of the babies survived except my father. They were either miscarriages or stillborn. Only one other baby lived to six months. She herself died giving birth to the last child.

My grandfather remarried when Papa was five. He remembered the wedding mainly because he drained the dredges of the guests' wine glasses and got drunk! Papa's stepmother was the sister of Uncle Hermann's wife. She was nice to him, which probably meant that she didn't bother him much and he always remembered her fondly. When my father was a small boy, his father sent him to spend the summers in the village of Tostedt where his mother, Wilhelmina had come from and where her family still lived. He stayed with his mother's sister, Anna, and her family. Her husband was the village schoolmaster during the winter months and worked his farm during the summer. This was the only actual farming experience Papa ever had and was the basis of his buying the farm. It takes a lot of courage to embark on such a life-changing enterprise with no more experience than watching one's uncle as a young boy, but apparently Papa had been very observant and had a good memory. Either that or he was nuts! It must have been the former as everything worked out OK. Papa's mother's father, Hermann Sauermann, was a bookbinder in Tostedt, and my father often told me of sitting on the floor of the shop, while the old man was working, and reading the individual uncut pages of the books that his grandfather was binding. This entailed a lot of turning to read the pages in sequence, as they were sent as large sheets from the printer and had to be cut by the bookbinder, so that the pages lined up in the proper numerical order.

My parents and I visited Tostedt in 1954, and my father said it hadn't changed all that much except the thatched roofs were being removed to lower the insurance premiums. The house that Grandpa Sauermann built was still standing, except that there was now an orange tile roof. One of my father's cousins, Annelise, still lived there. I don't know any more about the Wentzels, my father's ancestors. It has always been assumed that they had, sometime in the distant past, emigrated to Hamburg, the big city, from some place in Bohemia. This is based only on the name "Wentzel" which is a fairly common given name in that area. Mama's father, Hans Ehrich, was born in Itzehoe, which was at that time part of Denmark, sometime around the 1840s. He was drafted into the Danish army at age 20. He always had good things to say about the Danes. It was while he was in their army that he was taught to read and write. The Danes lost the war with Prussia sometime during the 1860s, and all of Schleswig-Holstein became part of Germany. However, Grandpa Ehrich still could not live in peace. No, the Prussians had other plans. The Danish contingent was conscripted into the German army and was sent to fight France in 1870. After the defeat of France, Grandpa was sent home, but as he was now a German Citizen and no longer Danish, he decided to try his luck in Hamburg rather than remain in his village. He married and had a son Nicholas. Unfortunately, his wife died in childbirth and he was left to raise the baby on his own. He quickly remarried as that was the easiest way to get childcare. His second wife gave him five more children; Heinrich, Henrietta, Dora, Caroline and Wilhelmina. Wilhelmina died of polio. Then his second wife passed away. Now Grandpa had a whole flock of kids that needed care. That's when he married my Grandmother, Emma Margarethe Dorothea Piepgrass. She came from a farming family which lived somewhere in the neighborhood of Hamburg. He then fathered Hans, Emma, Johanna, Marie, Antonia and Else. Else fell out of a swing as a toddler and did not survive. As the story goes, the older children were heartbroken that their baby sister was gone and begged to have another. That's supposed to be why my mother came to be.

My father was always a very good student and got excellent grades in school. His Grandmother Wentzel kept insisting that he should be sent to the University, but my Grandfather, her son, always had the same reply, "The boy doesn't want to. He has some crazy idea that he wants to go to sea and someday be a captain. He'll find out soon enough what it's like!" So my Grandfather signed Papa up as an apprentice on a three-masted sailship. As the cabin boy he got all the unpleasant chores that the experienced seamen had learned to avoid. The ship's first stop after leaving Hamburg was London. He was appalled at the conditions. Ragged children were running in the streets, sweeping up after the horse-drawn vehicles. They were collecting the horse droppings to sell to farmers to earn a few pennies to survive. Conditions must have been pretty terrible to shock a fourteen-year-old boy. He did not like London. It was still a very dirty city in 1906.

The ship's next stop was Vera Cruz. Papa liked Mexico. In later years, he said he wouldn't mind visiting again, but because of his war wound, he would not be able to eat Mexican food, therefore would be compelled to take with him an awful lot of sandwiches, a really giant picnic lunch! Wouldn't be practical. After Mexico, the ship sailed south to Cape Horn to the unbelievably cold stormy weather that exists there, probably all year round! In this frigid weather, his fingers all became frost-bitten and remained sort of strange-looking for the rest of his life. It is hard to believe that he could do the delicate work that he did with fingers that looked like sausages! Life at sea was not at all the way he had pictured it. In addition to the cold, foul weather, the food was barely edible. After the cargo, guano (bird droppings, centuries old) had been shoveled aboard at the Chilean islands were it was found and the ship had made the miserable voyage back to Hamburg, Papa quit.

He was next apprenticed to a furrier. This turned out to be just a delivery boy's job, also unsatisfactory, so he didn't stay there very long. He was then apprenticed to a locksmith which was somewhat more interesting, but still not really satisfying, so once again, Papa quit. When he came to his father and said he wanted to be apprenticed to a jeweler, Grandpa said, "Fine, do what you want, but I have signed for you on three apprenticeships, and now that you are sixteen, you can sign up for yourself! I'm through!" So my father did just that and finally found his calling

My mother, meanwhile, was sent at age 14 to work as a maid for some wealthy people. As the mistress was also named "Margaret", my mother was told right off, that it was impossible for her to use the same name, so she had to get another name at once, or get another job! She chose "Margo" and married quite young, probably to get out of that household. She had a baby at nineteen, my sister Lori. The fellow Mama married was an itinerant lithographer, named Richard Wolf and the family traveled all over Europe; Russia, Scandanavia, Belgium and probably a number of other countries as well. My sister was born in Stockholm. When the First World War broke out, they were in Belgium and had to flee back to Germany. Their marriage broke apart shortly thereafter. Mama became a nurse because of the great need for nurses for the war wounded. She must have learned nursing on the job because she never spoke of having gone to school for it. She wouldn't have been able to afford the tuition, anyway. She survived this way, supporting herself and her daughter, who was farmed out to relatives, as Mama had to live at the hospital. Luckily, she had a lot of them. My father said after they had been married for years, he kept meeting new ones!

Mr. Wolf died in the Spanish Flu Pandemic of 1918, in which fifty million people lost their lives, worldwide, and 500,000 in the United States alone! It was surprising that so many of the victims were young or middle-aged people, supposedly in the prime of their lives, rather than the very young or the very old. A year later, Mama met my father, who was recuperating in the hospital from his last wound, a very serious abdominal wound. He finally recovered well enough to be sent home, and they were married in 1921. I guess I can say I owe my existence to the Spanish Flu!

They had been married for a few years, my sister was a teen-ager, about ready to become an apprentice, to a milliner, and therefore was almost considered a grown-up, when my mother decided it would be nice to have another child. My father did not think very much about this idea. He was still very nervous and easily upset at this time. Today, it would probably be called "Post-traumatic Stress". But in those days it was just considered nervousness. He felt that a nice quiet house suited him just fine. From what he had heard about babies, they did not add up to peace and quiet. But my mother persisted and I was born in 1925. To my father's surprise, I wasn't a boy! How could that have happened? As he had finally agreed to a baby, he felt that at least it should have been a boy. This really was not right! But as I was a quiet baby and didn't disturb him very much, he finally stopped complaining. In later years, Mama said to me, "Don't mind him, he is really so proud of you!" This was good to hear, even though I had suspected as much. We were not a demonstrative family, but I always knew that he loved me.

CHAPTER 31

SOCIAL INSECURITY

We were never a church-going family. My mother said her mother attended church on Good Friday, but never recalled her going at any other time. She always felt that a person's good deeds spoke for themselves and what was in their hearts and their relationships with other people was what really mattered to God. Sticking to the quirks and rituals of organized religion was unimportant. However when she and I were still in the hospital, a minister came around and persuaded her to have me baptized. She thought, he seems like such a nice man, so what could it hurt? and agreed. My father was not favorably impressed, having always been an agnostic, but he, too, could not come up with any serious objections.

As it turned out, it did no harm at all. In fact, 62 years later, it was a great help to me. My birth certificate, for reasons unknown, had never been returned to my mother by the American Consul in Hamburg when we applied for immigration papers. For sixty-two years, I got along just fine without it. I got my enemy alien booklet, citizenship papers, driver's license and voter's registration and a passport, all without a birth certificate, only my original German passport, dated 1928, served as proof of birth and date and place of same. However, applying for Social Security turned out to be a whole different matter! This involved an actual cash outlay by the Federal Government, and they were not about to pay out to a person, who as far as they knew had never been born, or anyway could not prove it! I had to go back to Miami from Key Largo a number of times, continually bringing in more documents. I brought in my U.S. passport from 1964, my U.S. citizenship Papers, my Enemy Alien Booklet, a copy of the ship's manifest showing that I had been a passenger on the "New York" in 1928, and my German passport. As I mentioned before, my mother saved every thing! Still they weren't satisfied until they saw the earlier mentioned baptismal certificate. "Oh," they said, 'What's this?" I explained to them and they made a note of the date, 4-23-25. Of course, it was printed in German and unreadable to them, but it had my name and the date. Something was hand written on the bottom of the sheet. It was carefully scrutinized and I was asked, "Is that the Pastor's signature?" I said, "Yes, of course." They were finally satisfied! I would never, ever mention that it was the name of the Pastor's church handwritten at the bottom and his name did not appear on it at all!

CHAPTER 32

EDUCATION

I have only attended primary schools in two states, Maryland and New York. In each of these states there was a concerted effort to convince the students that they were getting the best possible education available in these United States. I have to believe that they were both wrong! When we first arrived back in New York, in 1937, my mother went to enroll me in the seventh grade, as I had successfully completed six years of elementary school in Maryland. The Board of Education of N.Y.C., in the form of the person in charge of admissions refused to believe that I could possibly keep up with the New York children who had the benefit of six years of a New York education. They actually wanted me to repeat the sixth grade! My mother was furious! How could they even think of doing such a thing? "Disgraceful," she said, "Margaret must be put in the seventh grade, she has been on the honor roll for six years." Of course, Mama did not mention that there were multiple grades taught by one teacher in one room. At least it wasn't a one room school house, there were three! She also didn't tell them that when I was eleven, a test had been given to fifth, sixth, and seventh graders which was actually an admissions test for the University of Maryland. Why, I have no idea, but it turned out that I was the only kid to pass this test. I was not especially impressed, and probably did not even mention it to my parents. At age eleven, I couldn't have cared less about college! That, of course, changed but I also was not impressed much by the University of Maryland, either. Imagine, an eleven-year old passing their entrance exam without any preparations. I hope they have raised their standards since! I'm sure they have.

They finally, very reluctantly, relented. "Well, she is from out-of-state, she will undoubtedly have a very hard time with the class work." "Try her", said Mama. So they agreed, but on their terms. I was enrolled in 7A 6, in with the dummies. Thanks to my mother's persistence, I worked my way up to be able to graduate with the rapid advance class which would have made me eligible to attend Hunter High, which would have insured admission to Hunter College, a free city college, but the depression was still in full swing, so college was not an option for me. I enrolled in Julia Richman High because of their excellent commercial courses.

Recently, I saw a magazine ad for brochures about Dorchester County, Md. This was the area where our farm had been located, so I sent for them. I was amazed to find, among many brochures extolling the virtues of a vast number of restaurants and hotels in and near Cambridge, the County Seat, one called "Finding a way to Freedom", which gave directions for a driving tour through Caroline and Dorchester Counties, following the path of the "Underground Railroad." This had been a network of anti-slavery sympathizers who had helped escaped slaves to reach freedom across the Mason-Dixon Line. Foremost among them was Harriet Tubman, who had been born into slavery in an area quite close to where we later lived. I never knew this, it had never been mentioned in school, nor did I know that in the 1850's, about 4000 African-Americans were enslaved here, in Dorchester County. Well, so much for the quality and extent of a Maryland education!

CHAPTER 33

THE END OF CHILDHOOD, 1943

Life had become relatively uneventful for us in Astoria, as we had no direct connections to any service men or their relatives. My girlfriends did not have older brothers, just pesky younger ones. At some point when I was in high school, the building we lived in was sold and we had to move. Not very far, just across the street and down to the end of the block where Crescent Street intersected Hoyt Ave., so we still lived on Crescent St. My father thought the place was very nice. He could use the entire ground floor for a workshop, even though it had been condemned by the Board of Health for human habitation because of dampness. Not only mould and mildew grew there, but actual mushrooms as well. The landlord had no objections to his working there, and did not charge, so this was fine with Papa. At least there were no curtains to catch fire! The adjacent side yard had never been developed, so it was an empty lot, just waiting for my father to plant vegetables to fill it up. He was happy, my mother was, too, but it meant a lot more work for her, to pick, prepare, and can all of these veggies. They really did come in very handy to supplement our diets in wartime. Mama also liked the place because it came with an electric refrigerator and a gas range. There was no central heating, but for twenty-five dollars a month, it was still a pretty good deal. Despite the extra work my mother had with the vegetables, it was certainly not comparable to her work load on the farm. Sewing clothes for herself and me was a necessity, but now she had some time to do needlework, which she loved. She embroidered four or five tablecloths for my sister and later for me. She also found the time to crochet a beautiful bedspread for me! I shall cherish it always!

There was one more apartment upstairs, occupied by a very old lady and her son. The old lady was extremely deaf, and the son had become a drug addict during the First World War, the first addict I had ever heard of! We would all sit on the front porch in the evening and the old lady would regale us with tales about the "Good old days" of her youth, when she would take the ferry across the East River to Manhattan, where she worked. Sometimes, the river froze over and horse-drawn carriages were put to use to transport travelers across the frozen river! She also never tired of reminiscing about the "Blizzard of 1888." These had been the high points of her life. She was so deaf that she never heard the air-raid sirens, so the air-raid warden had to come up the stairs to bang on her door to alert her to put out her lights. I guess she must have felt the vibrations of the knocking. She couldn't have heard him!

In 1943 I graduated from Julia Richman High School, which was an all-girls school at the time. I had reasonably good grades, being in the highest 10 percentile. However, as I had not taken the academic course, thanks to my Guidance Counselor, I was not able to attend any City College, which would have been free. My parents had given me a typewriter for my sixteenth birthday, so now I could handle my family's correspondence in a very professional way! My father was still looking to find a more suitable job, so I got to write the letters of application for him. After all, I was attending an American school and taking typing classes, so I was certainly qualified! One of these jobs was in Providence, Rhode Island, with a watch making firm, Bulova, I think, but due to his lack of citizenship, they were unable to hire him, even though they would have liked to. "Too bad," he said, "Now I can't pay you the five dollars you would have earned if I had gotten the job!" But for that quirk of fate, I could have spent my teen years in Rhode Island. My father did finally find a much better job. In fact, after the war, he actually had two jobs, one teaching returning G.I.s jewelry making, in one of the many so-called technical schools that had sprung up to take advantage of government's education programs to retrain returning veterans. However, most of his students had no real interest in learning, they were in it for the monetary benefits and learning to make subway tokens, so that they could ride for free! It proved to be too much work, and not rewarding enough to teach mostly unmotivated students. He quit that job and concentrated on fabricating custom work for quality retailers like Tiffany, Cartier and other high-end stores.

After graduation, my Guidance Counselor sent me to apply for work at Guardian Life Insurance Co. It was a boring job and the pay was only minimal, $35 every two weeks. I stayed with it all summer, not spending any money at all except subway fare. Lunch I brought from home. On Mondays, Wednesdays and Fridays, the firm gave us ice cream for dessert. On Tuesdays and Thursday, we only got cookies which were so tasteless that I brought them home to my dog, who liked any gift. After I left Guardian Life, I still had to give my dog something when I came home. We settled on dog biscuits. Probably had pretty much the same flavor! I had planned to use my savings to go to N.Y.U., but the $60 I had saved up was not nearly enough. I then got a job working for an accountant, who unbeknownst to me, only hired young girls straight out of high school or with very limited experience and after a very short training session, sent them out to his unsuspecting clients to do their books. If the girls were conscientious, everything would be fine. If not, he would just send out another girl. They even prepared the taxes for these people without supervision! This job paid even less than the insurance company, $12.50 a week, but I thought the experience would be worth what I had lost in salary. I did get a lot of experience there, I must admit, it certainly helped me get my next job. In retrospect, I feel sorry for his clients, but I guess in some instances, you get what you pay for. This worked out OK for me until tax time came around and I was expected to work overtime at half my regular low rate! This was absurd, all day Saturday and Sunday at half-time instead of time and a half! I quit!

Meanwhile, I had seen an ad for Cooper Union in the N.Y. Times which read "Get a College Education in Art, Free." This was for me! I had always been drawing and painting all my life, so I applied and was given a test to see if I qualified. I didn't think I had passed the test, because was difficult for me to draw figures just like that, nothing to copy or anything! After a few weeks, the notice came. I was hesitating before opening it, but, surprise, I had passed! This was the beginning of my new life. I would be attending Cooper Union School of Art at night for four years, twelve hours a week!

ABOUT THE AUTHOR

After graduating from Cooper Union in 1947, I was employed by a number of display firms, fabricating displays for department stores. The most interesting of these was designing and producing papier mache clothes for six-foot tall pre-formed papier mache bunnies. Display work was very seasonal, however, so I felt that I would be better off with steadier employment. I became a bookkeeper instead, as I had taken a commercial course in high school, and eventually became office manager. After I married, Julius and I moved to Long Island, where we lived for twenty-two years. After my mother passed away, we moved to Florida, along with my Dad, so that we could be close to my sister in Tamarac. We relocated to Key Largo after both of them passed away. We continued to live there for nearly twenty years, until my husband died and I moved to Century Village, here in Pembroke Pines. This is a very nice retirement community and I enjoy being here. I have a splendid view from my fourth floor condo, overlooking the golf course with its lakes and the many birds that live there. I keep very busy, making friends, attending classes, and being a member of the Camera Club. Another plus is living so close to Julius's sister, Dorothy. Once a week I volunteer at Adopt-A-Stray. I take care of the cats and welcome visitors who are interested in adoption and give them an opportunity to react with the cats. (See picture) My previous writing experiences consist of "Letters to the Editor" and my monthly contributions to "The Cooppa Guardian", our Century Village paper.